The Book Of Entertaining At Home

By Maureen Molé

A contemporary guide to hosting successful parties, from brunches to formal dinners, including:

extending invitations

menu planning

styles of service

introductions

dealing diplomatically with guests

party preliminaries

The Book of
Entertaining
& At Home

MAUREEN MOLÉ

Cornerstone Library

NEW YORK

Published by Cornerstone Library, Inc.,
a Simon & Schuster subsidiary of
Gulf & Western Corporation

Simon & Schuster Building
Rockefeller Center
1230 Avenue of the Americas
New York, New York 10020

Cornerstone Library and colophon are trademarks
of Simon & Schuster, registered in the U.S.
Patent and Trademark Office.

ISBN: 0-346-12397-6

Centerpieces in photographs by
Doris Shannon of Colonial House
Of Flowers, Ridgewood, New Jersey.

To my mother,
Carmel Altomare, an exceptional hostess

In acknowledgement I would like to thank—

Ron, my husband, for his understanding and his sense of humor; for sharing with me his precise knowledge of words; for his willingness to assume the role of mother at times (as well as father); and for being an encouraging friend to me at all times . . .

Ingrid Russell, my editor, for her caring; for contributing her knowledge of the subject in addition to her clarity of thought and perceptive editing; and for her ability to be friend and listener as well as editor . . .

and special thanks as well to Patricia Barrett, Dick Brunner, Rosemary Brunner, Tom Hunter, Audrey Miller, Ray Murphy and Doris Shannon.

To my daughters, Marissa and Noelle, I would like to express the hope that they will understand that a woman can be an author, or whatever she wants to be, in addition to being a mother.

❦ Contents

1 ❦ A CONTEMPORARY PHILOSOPHY TO HOME ENTERTAINING

2 ❦ PARTY PRELIMINARIES

3 ❦ MENU PLANNING

4 ❦ IT'S NOT ONLY WHAT BUT HOW

5 ❦ TABLE SETTINGS: THE STAGE FOR THE PARTY

6 ❦ IT'S THE LITTLE THINGS

7 ❦ DINNER PARTIES

8 ❦ THE LOGISTICS OF SERVICE

9 ❦ COCKTAIL PARTIES

10 ❧ A POTPOURRI OF PARTIES

11 ❧ DEALING DIPLOMATICALLY WITH GUESTS

12 ❧ WHEN YOU ARE THE GUEST

❦1

A Contemporary Philosophy for Home Entertaining

❦ Successful Parties

Aim for success at all your parties. Successful parties are when everyone has a good time *including the party giver*. This book gives specific guidelines to help you, the party giver, enjoy your own parties and maximize your guests' enjoyment as well. The following factors, and many others, will stack the deck in your favor—advance preparation, organization, fine food, good drinks, interesting people, and gracious hosts.

The only criterion you should use when judging your party's success is, "Did everyone at the party, *including me,* have a good time?"

❦ Your Entertaining Identity

Determine the style of entertaining that suits you best. Different strokes for different folks. Once you establish your own entertaining identity, you will feel capable and confident to handle the party you are about to plan.

Your party should be *you.* Plan a party that is consistent with your personality and one at which your own circle of friends will feel comfortable. A party should reflect the party giver. If you have a keen interest in music, then plan to have music at your party. If you enjoy cooking, then plan a five-course dinner for your special friends. On the other hand, if you are unsure of your culinary talents, plan easy recipes or buy prepared foods. You might prefer the casualness of outdoor entertaining with the convenience of using paper napkins. Or, if your manner is a bit more formal, you might want to bring out your damask or lace. Don't try to be what you are not. Don't attempt the insurmountable. Understate rather than overstate. But, be yourself.

Cathy used to shudder at the thought of giving a large cocktail party. The prospect of preparing an interesting variety of hors d'oeuvres, precisely regulating the timing in the kitchen, and being calm and congenial with thirty guests all at one time traumatized her. She would rather clean out the attic or the silverware drawer than deal with the organization required to entertain a crowd. Nevertheless, she did not forsake home entertaining altogether. She discovered her individual style and invited a small group of six for cheese, crackers, and wine. She managed very well.

Where you live, how you live, and what you enjoy will give you a unique entertaining identity. A woman living in a spacious suburban home plans one type of party; a woman living in a city apartment another. A young man who is a gourmet cook and a collector of expensive wines plans a party quite different from an older gentlemen living on a fixed income. No one type of party is better than the next. Do what suits your style.

Assess your lifestyle realistically. Evaluate the available space in your home, but don't let a lack of space become an insurmountable obstacle. Entertain as many people as you feel comfortable with. If you live in a matchbox apartment, a Sunday brunch for twenty-four is out of the question; a small intimate get-together isn't.

Consider your budget. Let's face it—most of us don't have an endless amount of money to spend on our parties. Set a reasonable party budget and plan within its framework; you can still produce an effective party. The tally of costs does not determine a party's success. Even millionaires can have dull parties. Be practical about your financial limitations and party costs and plan accordingly.

Whether your style is lush and lavish or modest and moderate, finding your entertaining identity will naturally help develop the confidence you need to plan an outstanding party of which you can be proud.

❧ *Excuses, Excuses*

Rid yourself of whatever happens to be your excuse for not having a party. Anyone can plan a party and a successful one at that. Face the fact that many excuses are nothing more than just that—excuses. Here are some popular ones:

Mary Jean is a career woman. She's out of the house from 8:00 A.M. to 6:00 P.M. She says, "Entertaining is not for me. I don't have the time." However, with advance preparation and organization, Mary Jean could find the time to entertain if she really wanted to.

Frank has a million excuses. He says, "I don't entertain at home because my apartment is too small, I don't have expensive china, and I'm not a very good cook." Frank is just plain scared. He should realize that just being himself is enough. He could entertain at home if he really wanted to.

Regina is a housewife and mother of three preschoolers. She says, "I can't plan a party because I'm too busy with my children." Hiring a babysitter in her own home the night of the party, or even including the children at the party would work for Regina if she really wanted to entertain.

Ellen is a free spirit. She says, "I don't have parties because I don't have to impress anyone." Ellen doesn't realize that giving a party is not a question of impressing, it's a question of caring. At a party you share yourself with others. The more you put into your party, the more you and your guests will get out of it.

So, the bottom line is, if you *really* want to entertain at home, you can.

❧ *"Please excuse the . . ."*

Give your guests the best of yourself. As long as you have prepared and done what is appropriate for the occasion, there's no reason to make excuses or call attention to something that might otherwise go unnoticed.

Don't apologize for your cooking ability or the modesty of your wine. The success or failure of a party does not depend on whether you serve hamburgers or beef Wellington; domestic jug wine or Château Lafite-Rothschild. Gourmet food and costly wine might add a pleasant plus to an elegant party, but they are not critical. Doing your best is more important.

Don't apologize for the size of your home, the unmatched dining room chairs or the way your home is decorated. The guests are invited to enjoy your company and to socialize with the other guests, not to critically evaluate your interior decorating skills or to count the cracks in the ceiling. Moreover, apologies for the wine or furnishings may embarrass your guests and make them uncomfortable.

You'll wait forever if you think you must finish all the remodeling or redecorating before you plan a party. Some people think that every pleat on every curtain must be perfect before they invite one guest to their home. Others can invite a houseful of people, have a flourishing party and all without any curtains on the windows. On the other hand, it is nice to plan a party to celebrate a finished household task, such as a new patio or a finished basement. The party provides the deadline and, of course, the incentive to complete the work on time.

Some hosts feel they must make excuses for the untidiness of their home, even if it's tidy. They feel compelled to explain, "Don't pay any attention to the mess." We rarely hear, "I spent all day cleaning the house, come in and notice." Both comments are unnecessary and boring.

Forget the excuses. New wallpaper and expensive wines don't make a party, people do.

❦Good Reasons To Stay At Home

People appreciate the personal touch and intimacy of home entertaining. The comfortable atmosphere in your own living room is much more conducive to a budding friendship than the communal surroundings of a public restaurant or hall. Some hosts might have the means to take friends to the most expensive restaurants, but gracious hospitality in your own home surpasses unlimited expense accounts.

Business entertaining at home is becoming more and more popular. Giving a *successful* party for the boss and his or her spouse certainly can't hurt the career of a rising young executive. Quite a few corporate deals have been negotiated over a homemade piece of apple pie and a glass of hot-buttered rum. Business entertaining at home makes a "client" feel more like a "friend" and can facilitate business transactions. Many traveling businessmen attest that they prefer the congenial surroundings of a guest room in the home of an associate to the lonely setting of an unfamiliar hotel room.

Whether you're entertaining business guests, relatives or the neighbors, having a party at home allows you to express yourself artistically. It's your chance to be as creative and innovative as you like. Parties at home resemble those childhood handmade birthday cards for Mom. Didn't she always seem to prefer the ones you designed yourself? Even though your card was not as professional as Hallmark's, it was still better to Mom. Your party, like that birthday card, is a unique self-expression and creative achievement. It may not be as professional as a catered affair, but it makes up for it with thoughtfulness, warmth, and individuality.

And when all is said and done, home entertaining is usually less expensive than going out.

ℰ *What To Do With The Children*

Recognize that your children do exist. You can't very well sweep them under the rug, stuff them in an already over-crowded closet, or camouflage them as one would a worn sofa by shrouding them with a throw cloth.

Children should not be considered obstacles that prevent parents from entertaining at home. One of the most frequent excuses that couples offer for not inviting guests is that their children, toddlers or teenagers, are a hindrance. Indeed, there are factors to be considered, but there are workable solutions, too.

First, establish a positive attitude. Make up your mind that you are going to have a party, even though taking care of the children might require a little more planning, organization and patience. If you start out with a defeatist attitude, you will surely be defeated.

If you decide to include the children at your party, then organize an afternoon gathering which they can enjoy. Plan an outdoor barbecue, a Christmas caroling party, or a treasure hunt. Even at dinner and cocktail parties some participation is possible, if it is well planned.

If you prefer not to have the children attend an evening party at all, arrange to have the guests arrive *after* the children's bedtime. If you are worried about juggling your time and attention between the children and the guests, arrange to have a babysitter come to your house to care for the children in another area of the house while you are busy with the guests. Or make an arrangement with friends to invite your children overnight to their home. You can return the favor the next time your friends have a party.

Another option is to allow the children to greet the guests for a short time. Decide beforehand whether or not you want them to help when the guests arrive. Some teenagers might prefer to keep out of sight, and if you have toddlers, you might prefer to keep them out of sight. But you can enlist the aid of children in the in-between age group. They can be your helpers.

Explain the details of the party to your children. Tell them whom you have invited and what you have planned. Instruct them how to be hospitable little hosts themselves. Youngsters can take the guests' coats, distribute cocktail napkins and even serve some hors d'oeuvres. Then, after a reasonable amount of time, the children should excuse themselves from the party.

One evening Deborah was permitted to stay awake and greet some business guests that her parents were entertaining. She was forewarned to be on her best behavior and was told that she could distribute the coasters for the cocktail glasses. As a guest sipped his martini, Deborah cautioned him with all the politeness she could muster, "You better not spill that drink on the couch or my mother will kill you."

For the most part, children rarely utter such embarrassing remarks. Talk to your children beforehand and discuss the manner in which you expect them to behave. You'll be surprised to see that many young people will participate successfully in the family's home entertaining.

❧ Etiquette

View etiquette in its proper perspective. Good manners are simply a matter of common courtesy and consideration of other people. The word "etiquette" need not conjure up negative thoughts of pretentiousness, stuffiness and snobbery. Certain guidelines are useful and necessary. Approach them with a positive attitude.

Basic table setting rules are beneficial. They ensure attractiveness and uniformity on the table, as well as maximizing the comfort and convenience of the guests. For example, forks are traditionally placed to the left of the plate. Imagine the needless chatter if forks were placed haphazardly on the table and guests had to determine which fork was whose. The rule's usefulness is evident. Similarly, try to respond promptly to written invitations and be on time for parties.

The nonconformists who disregard society's "rules" are sometimes nothing but downright inconsiderate people—the ones who call at 7:00 P.M. to cancel your dinner invitation at 8:00 P.M. because they don't feel "up to it," the ones who arrive an hour late for dinner, or the ones who forget to come altogether. On the other hand, believing in "rules for rules' sake" is just as foolish as ignoring all good manners. Some people worry if the maid walks into the dining room holding the first-course platter in her right hand instead of her left. (Most people don't even have maids to worry about.) Rules indicating whether the serving spoon should be placed *next to* or *in* the condiment dish or if a plate should be passed clockwise or counterclockwise are "rules for rules' sake."

If what the etiquette books says makes you feel uncomfortable, then forget it. But not at the expense of someone else. The contemporary approach is to view etiquette with practicality and common sense. Consideration of others, politeness, and good judgment are foremost.

ℰ *Hiring Helpers*

Consider hiring some help if you are planning a large party even if you usually do everything yourself. The helper doesn't have to be a professional maid or butler either. (If you want to hire a professional helper or caterer by all means do, but this book is geared for those of you who want to do it mainly on your own.)

Eileen and Ken hired the teenager who usually babysits for their children. I know a hostess who called the local youth employment service, while another placed an ad in her local newspaper in search of teenage assistance. For a large cocktail party, the teenager can collect the used glasses and dishes, empty the ash trays, restock the bar, and help pass the hors d'oeuvres. For a buffet, your helper can stay in the kitchen and load the dishwasher, wash the pots, and keep the room in order. These tasks are not difficult for teenagers, and many of them are pleased to earn the extra spending money. (Just remind them to dress appropriately.)

If you want to employ a bartender, you needn't hire a professional. A capable college student can do the job. But before you hire a bartender, consider the:

Advantages	Disadvantages
1. relieves the host and guests from mixing drinks	1. the cost
2. knows how to fix a variety of drinks	2. slows service because a bartender can mix only one drink at a time whereas guests can mix their own drinks simultaneously
3. makes drinks neither staggeringly strong nor watery and weak	3. slows service when the bartender also doubles as a waiter to serve the drinks
4. prevents waste since guests tend not to measure and may mix drinks that they won't consume	

Loretta and John told me that they attended a party with 50 other guests. The bartender mixed the drinks in the kitchen and served them on a tray to each guest. An hour passed and some guests still didn't have their first cocktail. There obviously should have been two bartenders. Having too little help is as bad as no help at all. To hasten the service, the bartender at that party should have stayed behind the bar and simply handed a drink to each guest upon request.

Many hosts feel that the worst part of having a party is cleaning up afterwards. If this is your nightmare, then hire someone to do it or to help you do it. Whether the job is setting up, serving, clearing or cleaning up, hiring a helper can ease the pain.

❦ Good Reasons For Partying

Give a party for any reason that suits your fancy. Let your imagination and even your sense of humor lay the foundation. Have a New Year's Eve party in July and an indoor beach party in February. Don't limit yourself to the conventional.

Many parties are given for the customary celebration of birthdays and anniversaries, but a twist of the traditional can broaden your party horizon. Have a "Jack Benny" Birthday Party for your friend who is eternally thirty-nine. For your intellectual friends, celebrate the birthday of Albert Einstein, March 14. Invite geniuses to the party, of course. Plan to commemorate the wedding anniversary of Martha and George Washington, January 6; the opening of New York City's subway, September 10; or the anniversary of the first flight of the Wright Brothers, December 17.

The season or a holiday can dictate a gala event. Give a party in celebration of the splendor of autumn or a spring party in honor of Mother Nature. Have an Easter egg hunt or a Christmas tree decorating party. For a Valentine's Day party, ask the guests to bring something each loves besides their spouses or dates, of course.

Plan a party to get yourself through a crisis or a difficult situation. An aunt of Beth's was scheduled for surgery. Beth was quite concerned, although the doctors assured her that the operation was routine. I told her to turn those hours of useless worry into something more constructive. I suggested that she plan a party to take place after her aunt recuperated. Whenever Beth's thoughts strayed in the direction of needless worry, she planned the guest list, menu, and decorations for her party. Her aunt recovered quickly, and Beth thanked me afterwards for the suggestion. By the way, she had a very successful party, too.

A party is a great cure for a broken heart, a remedy for loneliness, and an all purpose antidote for a severe case of the blahs.

Suggested Party Themes and Ideas

Kentucky Derby Party
Old Family Photograph
   Swap Party
Gone With the Wind Party
Come As You'd Like To Be
   Party (instead of Come
   As You Are)

Plant Party
Cookie Swap Party
Share the Cooking Party
Vacation Photos Party (I'll
   look at yours, if you look
   at mine)
Pot Luck Supper

Pre-Football Game Party
After-Theatre Party
Christmas Caroling Party
Christmas Tree Decorating
    Party
Roaring 20s Swim Party
50s Dance Party
World Series Party
Great Gatsby Party
Mardi Gras
Las Vegas Night Party

Toga Party
Treasure Hunt
Astrology Party (invite
    only compatible signs)
Indoor Beach Party (in
    February)
New Year's Eve Party (in
    July)
Spring Party (In Honor Of
    Mother Nature)

Children's Parties

Easter Egg Hunt
Circus Party
Crazy Hat Party
Sesame Street Party
Come As Your Favorite
    Nursery Rhyme or
    Cartoon Character Party
Piñada Party
Cookie Baking Party

Peanut Hunt Party
Monster Party
Western Party
Book Swap Party
Bicycle Decorating Party
Baby Shower (for your
    dog's puppies)
Birthday Party (for your
    cat)

❧2

Party Preliminaries

❧ Cooking Up The Guest List

Combine interesting people to form the perfect recipe for a successful party. The skill of mixing people is just as important as assembling ingredients to make a delicious cake or a tasty cocktail. Even before the food and drinks are served, your ability to combine people will be demonstrated.

Invite people who will be entertaining and who bring out the best in each other. They don't necessarily have to know one another.

To animate the evening, your guest list should blend different types of stimulating people. A party would be dull if you served only one type of food and one kind of drink. If you invite people in only one profession, it can be equally boring. Too much "shoptalk" lends an everyday quality that any party can easily do without.

Combine the sexes, too. Have a good balance of men and women but don't give a second thought to having an extra male or female guest. Parties consisting of all couples, all the time, are passé.

If friends can predict the entire guest list before a party, you know you're headed for a humdrum evening. So add a dash of surprise by mixing old friends with new ones. Invite older people as well as younger, talkers as well as listeners, shy as well as outgoing people. Ideally, invite people you genuinely want to be with and entertain.

Sometimes business situations and family obligations dictate a guest list. When you are obliged to invite a business associate who talks incessantly or an uncle who smokes a deadly cigar, make the best of it. You'll emerge as an accomplished host if you can deal with a guest list that is less than optimal.

However, don't invite catastrophe. The worst guest list of all is the one drawn up for a big "Pay-Off" party. The hosts invite everyone they feel socially obligated to, that is, anyone who has issued them an invitation in the past year or two. The growing guest list begins to look more like a Christmas card list. This type of party is destined for failure before it begins. The planning and work are usually overwhelming for the hosts, and the guests feel like cattle rather than people.

Planning a guest list can be as delicate as making a soufflé. No recipe is foolproof and there's usually a risk involved. Use your best judgment, because only you know your own friends. If you use discretion, more than likely your combination of guests will whip up into a delicious party.

✌ *Extending Invitations*

Extend your party invitations far enough in advance so that your prospective guests will be available. How much in advance is difficult to define. Some people's social calendars run a month or two in advance, while others prefer to plan their social engagements weekly. The general rule is to send written invitations about four weeks before a party. Invitations to small parties (less than twelve) are sometimes telephoned two or three weeks before, while invitations to formal affairs or holiday parties can be sent five to six weeks in advance.

Let us consider written vs. telephoned invitations. For a small party, you may prefer to extend your invitations informally by telephone. However, if you do use the telephone, it is more time consuming and you run several risks. You could be delayed by a busy signal or no answer at all. If the person answers, the time might be inopportune. The correct date, time, and address of the party might be inadvertently misunderstood or not even written down. And you don't always get an immediate answer, so additional telephoning is involved.

If you do telephone your invitations, it is advisable to follow up with a written reminder one week before the party. I learned that lesson the time I planned a surprise birthday party for my husband, Ron. I telephoned all the invitations several weeks beforehand. The party was to be on a Sunday at 6:30 P.M. A week before the party, I was speaking to Barbara, one of the guests, and she said, "See you on Saturday at 6:30." I said, "No, the party is on Sunday." Then Dorothy, another guest, said, "See you Sunday at 6:00." I said, "No, 6:30." I immediately sat down and wrote written reminders to all the guests.

Written invitations are faster and more definite. You offer a record of pertinent information that can be referred to as the date of the party draws near. An R.S.V.P. should be included. Adding a telephone number after the R.S.V.P. was once considered incorrect according to the rules of etiquette. However, it is now becoming accepted because, in general, written replies are no longer expected. So, including your telephone number saves guests the time of looking it up.

"Regrets Only," which also was considered incorrect, is becoming popular because many people don't bother to respond to invitations anyway. "Regrets Only" means that only guests who *cannot* attend the party must call the host. Now, even the etiquette books have recognized its frequent use. The rationale seems to be that hosts don't need to speak to guests who are coming. Personally, I think "Regrets Only" is a poor idea, except, perhaps, for a party of fifty people when you don't want to be inundated with calls. But then you forfeit the opportunity of filling in your guests about the party. Most of the time a telephone call confirming an invitation is very important. It confirms that a guest has received the invitation and it also gives the host or hostess an opportunity to brief the guest further. There is always more to a party than date, time and place.

❧ *Briefing The Guests*

Offer your guests as much information as possible about your party. Whether you are telephoning the invitations to everyone on the guest list or guests are calling you in response to a written invitation, use this time to supply them with the pertinent details. Surprises may not always be pleasant ones.

FOOD   If you have sent written invitations that indicate dinner, you can reiterate, "We will have a buffet dinner at 8:00." If your invitation is not for dinner, don't be embarrassed. Simply say, "We're looking forward to seeing you at 7:00 for some wine and cheese " Or, "Please come after dinner from nine o'clock on for drinks. We'll be having a midnight snack later in the evening." The important thing is to let your guests know whether you intend serving a meal (or its equivalent) or simply a nibble.

Al accepted a telephone invitation to a party. Both he and his wife, Rosalie, were invited. Although he was unsure if they were invited to dinner, he was too embarrassed to ask. So, Al and Rosalie just assumed that it was a dinner invitation. They arrived at the party at 8:00 P.M. By 10:00 P.M., after they had consumed the entire contents of the potato chip bowl and the avocado dip, they realized their guess had been wrong.

Misunderstandings are not limited to telephone conversations. Frank received a store-bought invitation with "Cocktail Buffet" printed on the cover. He wondered what type of food would be served. Unfortunately, there are no precise definitior s for some party titles. Cocktail buffet to some people m(ns a dinner served buffet style and to others it means some snacks will be served. He said the only thing he was certain about was that he would have a cocktail. As the invitation stated, "Regrets Only," Frank was hesitant about phoning his hostess. He scrutinized the cover of the invitation. It pictured a carafe of wine and assorted cheeses. "Just snacks," he thought, "no dinner." When he arrived at the party with a satisfied appetite, he discovered his assumption was wrong. The point to consider here is that store-bought, fill-in-the-blank invitations might have artwork or printing that is misleading. Therefore, it's best not to use them. Second, as I mentioned before, "Regrets Only" has its disadvantages. Third, certain terms are ambiguous. Avoid needless embarrassment on your part and that of your guests—be specific in your invitations, written or telephoned.

FOOD PREFERENCES For a dinner party, if you are concerned about fussy eaters and are hesitant to prepare *escargots* or frogs' legs, use a pre—party telephone conversation to obtain their food preferences. [See "Dieting Guests and Fussy Eaters" in chapter 11.] In the case of a guest of honor you can ask, "Do you prefer seafood, meat, or poultry?" And then plan accordingly.

WHO AND HOW MANY Give the guests a general idea of who's coming to your party—that is, family, neighbors, co-workers or old school friends. This will satisfy their natural curiosity. Secrets may cause embarrassment if one friend assumes another is invited. For all they know your party could be an intimate gathering of six or a banquet for one hundred. Let them know what's in store.

DRESS Indicate the mode of dress for your party. (References to dress are never written on an invitation, unless, of course, it is black tie or a costume party.) However, if you speak to the guests beforehand, they usually appreciate some insight. First, eliminate the word "casual" from your party vocabulary. Maryella told me of her chagrin when she was invited for a "casual" summer patio party at a neighbor's home. She arrived in a red checked shirt and a neat pair of slacks, only to find the other guests elegantly attired. The hostess sported a smart pinafore and the host was decked out in an all-white linen suit. "Casual" can mean anything from dresses and suits to quite informal T-shirts and jeans. Rather than use the ambiguous word "casual" when extending an invitation, tell your guests the manner in which *you* will be dressed, specifically, jeans, skirts, dresses, or jackets and ties. Don't dictate to them, but convey the information for use as a guideline.

THEMES AND SPECIAL ACTIVITIES If there is a theme to your party or a special activity planned, be sure to inform your guests. Whether it's an evening of charades or dancing, a luau by the pool, or an afternoon of watching the Superbowl, tell your friends what's in store so they can be prepared.

Your guests will feel more comfortable about attending your party if you supply them with the little details beforehand.

❦ Organization: Coordinating The Confusion

Organize yourself. This is one of the most important prerequisites to a successful party. Remember, the party giver must enjoy the party, too. Being organized before the party will make *you* feel better about it. Sure, spur-of-the-moment parties might be fun for the guests, but you'll be unnerved. And impromptu parties are usually lacking the finer points that would have been included if the party giver had more time to prepare.

Establish a system within which you can work. Know what has to be done, when to do it and how long it takes. Budget your time. If you don't already do this, then practice. Notice how long it takes to prepare a recipe, to vacuum the house, to set the table and to get yourself dressed. Then allow extra time for the unexpected—a telephone call from a long-winded friend or a crisis with the children. As long as you can anticipate the time required for necessary chores and allow time for the unanticipated, you should be able to institute a system.

Allow a period of several days for shopping, cooking and cleaning. Don't try to do all these tasks the day of the party. Shop for most of the food a few days ahead, except for very perishable items. This will permit you to begin cooking in advance, too. Do heavy housecleaning a day or two before the party, so that only a touch-up is necessary before the guests arrive.

Don't try to do too much in one day. Allow time for rest and relaxation. Dora, a working woman, who likes to entertain says that when she does a little each day the preparation for the party doesn't seem so overwhelming. "The work seems to be less," she says, "and on the day of the party I'm always amazed at all I've accomplished."

Do as many jobs as you can think of beforehand so you can enjoy your party with the guests. You'll be surprised at the number of chores that needn't be done at the last minute. (see "Countdown Checklist" in this chapter.)

As Aggie explains, "I was a disorganized, jack-in-the-box hostess. Up and down, up and down, all through dinner. I got up to fill the salt shaker and then again to fill the sugar bowl. In addition to last-minute food preparation, I spent extra time in the kitchen searching for salad utensils and serving bowls. I was running back and forth from the kitchen to the dining room all night, doing things I could have done ahead of time." Aggie finally learned that being organized beforehand allows her to spend more time with her guests during the party. Now she even prepares the coffee in advance. When it's time to serve dessert, she leaves her guests for all of two seconds to plug in the electric coffee pot and returns quickly to the dining room.

There're no two ways about it, a successful party is a well-organized party.

❦ Party Record Book

Keep a party record book. Any notebook will do. Record the date, guest list, kind of party (buffet, dinner, cocktail, luncheon), and the menu. Even jot down the outfit you wore.

Keeping an accurate log will help your future menu planning. You can avoid serving the "same ol' " reliable main course to the same guests at a subsequent party. On the other hand, if you find a particular menu is a gastronomic success at one party, use those same recipes again for different guests. What can be better than an entire pretested menu? In addition, reviewing your diary will help recall dishes that you haven't prepared in months.

If you feel inclined, jot down some helpful tidbits about the party or even mistakes that you made. For example, "All the guests preferred decaffeinated coffee," or "Jack is allergic to chocolate, don't make chocolate cream pie for him anymore." These notes will assist you in planning future parties for the same guests.

Write down favorite foods or certain topics of conversation your guests seem to enjoy. This can be particularly effective in business entertaining. Fran's husband's boss spent an entire evening telling them how well his young son, Tommy, plays soccer. Fran wrote it in her record book. A year later, when Fran met him at the office Christmas party, she asked, "How is Tommy's soccer game?" The boss marveled at her memory.

At one of my parties, Judy tried apricot brandy for the first time and loved it. This item went into my book. Several months later an occasion arose when I wanted to bring a gift for Judy. She was delighted when I brought a bottle of apricot brandy.

Include some notes about the color scheme and theme. I know a meticulous host who even takes color photographs of his table settings and decorations and tapes them in his book.

If you are conscientious about recording, your party diary will become one of your most valuable possessions.

❦ *Lists, Lists, Lists*

Live by your lists. Once a chore to do or an item to buy is written down on paper, don't worry about it. Joan, a capable hostess explains, "Before a party my head isn't filled with a million things to do and buy. I put my thoughts on a list and I don't have to think about them anymore. I just have to remind myself not to lose the list."

Here's a list of important lists:

1. *Guest list.*
2. *Menu.*
3. *Food shopping list.* Don't leave anything to memory. Review each recipe and note each ingredient. Check the supply you already have at home and what you need to buy. Don't overlook staples like salt, sugar, eggs, and milk. Write everything down. You'll be sorry if you forget to buy the sour cream for the beef strogan-off, or even worse, the blueberries for the blueberry pie.
4. *Inventory checklist.* These are items to buy, rent, or borrow. (The last one should be the shortest.) Gather these accessories well before the party. There's no rea-son to wait until the day of the party to run to the store to buy cocktail napkins or to a neighbor's home to borrow a punch bowl.
5. *Do-beforehand list.* Write a list of things to do before the party and section it off on a daily basis. Tape the list to your refrigerator or keep it in some other handy place. Whenever you think of a task that needs to be done, jot it down.
6. *Day-of-the-party list.* Prepare a list of little things to do after most of the cooking, shopping, cleaning, and other chores have been completed. This list, more than likely, will include fine points that need attention but are sometimes overlooked because of a lack of time. (See sample list below.)

❦ The Day Of The Party

Relax on the day of the party. Most of the major chores, like shopping, cooking, and cleaning, have been taken care of al-ready.

This is the day to take care of particulars. A day to complete the finishing touches that are, unfortunately, neglected by hosts who wait for the last minute to prepare everything.

Arrange flowers. Put the final trimmings on some recipes.

Organize your kitchen and dining room. Freshen up the bathroom. Do touch-up cleaning.

Finish all the work early enough to allow for resting. This is just as important as cooking and cleaning. There's nothing worse than hosts who look like they'd rather be taking a nap than attending their own party.

Dress leisurely. Budget your time so you will be ready before the guests are expected to arrive.

Then, greet your guests glowing with the confidence and charm that has been cultivated by good planning and organization.

❦ Countdown Checklist

ONE MONTH BEFORE THE PARTY:

__ write the guest list
__ set a theme for the party
__ decide on the menu
__ write or telephone invitations
__ make decisions about table settings, color scheme, linens, and decorations
__ engage hired help

TWO WEEKS BEFORE THE PARTY:

Inventory Checklist—make arrangements to buy, rent or borrow:

__ linens
__ glasses
__ tableware
__ napkins
__ cocktail napkins
__ ice bucket
__ serving bowls and platters
__ serving utensils
__ cheese boards
__ coffee urn

— extra tables
— extra chairs
— punch bowl
— other accessories

ONE WEEK BEFORE THE PARTY:

— prepare a food shopping list
— order liquor, wine, soda, extra ice (or make it)
— send reminder notes to follow up telephoned invitations
— write out a menu card
— make place cards
— prepare a day-by-day list of things to do beforehand

A FEW DAYS BEFORE THE PARTY:

— do general housecleaning
— polish and wash necessary items
— food shop
— start advance cooking, if you haven't already
— order flowers

ONE DAY BEFORE THE PARTY:

— set the table
— tend to other decorations
— finish cooking
— gather serving platters and utensils
— fill salt and pepper shakers, and sugar bowl
— ready the coat closet with extra hangers
— rearrange furniture
— assemble other necessary equipment
— defrost food for tomorrow
— finish yesterday's chores or start tomorrow's

THE DAY OF THE PARTY:

— arrange flowers
— retouch cleaning
— put finishing touches on recipes

__ clear counter tops
__ set up server or sideboard
__ chill water and wine
__ prepare coffee in pot
__ prepare fireplace or barbecue, if necessary
__ set out potholders, trivets and dishcloths
__ put out clean ash trays
__ put out nonperishable foods
__ set up the bar
__ freshen up the bathroom (clean guest towels and fresh soap)
__ REST

❧3

Menu Planning

❧ Advance Preparation Only

Choose recipes that are designed to be prepared in advance so that you will feel confident and relaxed the day of your party. There's a tremendous selection of tasty dishes, from elegantly simple to exclusively gourmet, that can be done ahead of time. There's simply no reason to choose last-minute foods. Some cookbooks indicate the number of days ahead food can be prepared, cooked and frozen or, at least, prepared and then cooked the day of the party.

Stagger the cooking schedule. Work on the first course and dessert one day and the vegetables and main course another. Then you won't feel devastated on the day of the party since the majority of kitchen work will have been completed.

One organized hostess I know revels in the fact that on the day of her party she can relax at the community's swim club because she knows all of her cooking is done. Whether you want to go swimming, take a nap or tend to the finishing touches of your party, once all the food has been prepared, you'll feel relieved.

Stick with recipes that won't be ruined if they sit in a warm oven. Guests are not always prompt, some linger over cocktails and sometimes the unexpected happens. Rather than have the whole dinner ruined, anticipate the possibility of delay and use recipes that won't spoil if they have to wait to be served.

Select recipes that require a minimum of last-minute preparation, seasoning, or heating. Try to have only one dish per course that requires attention. For example, cornish hens and string beans amandine can be ready and waiting in a warm oven while you prepare the wild rice.

Serving food will become easier if you plan a menu properly. Joe complained, "I never enjoy my own dinner parties because I don't sit down to eat with the guests. I spend more time in the kitchen doing final preparations than I do with my guests. I feel like a *ghost* instead of a *host*." Joe finally discovered that he could spend more time in the dining room with his guests by preparing mostly dishes that can be kept warm until the guests arrive at the table. He eliminated from his party repertoire soufflés and other dishes that must be served immediately after cooking. Service became easier for him when the last-minute kitchen work was lessened.

Plan to do your cooking before the day of your party. With a minimum of last-minute preparation, you won't feel like the enemy has arrived when the first guests ring the doorbell.

❧ Painless Menus and Service

Do what is easiest for *you*. Undertake the attainable. Your party doesn't have to rival a White House gala. Plan a reasonable menu that *you* can serve effortlessly.

Build the menu around your forté. Everyone usually has one special recipe. Start with your best and fashion the rest of the menu around that. If you have an outstanding recipe for stuffed pork chops, use that as your basis. Then decide on the other dishes. Or begin with the guest of honor's favorite dish (learn what it is from a pre—party telephone conversation). If he or she has a fancy for fish, select your choicest seafood recipe and go on from there.

If you want to keep your sanity, plan only *one* complicated or time-consuming dish. If you're energetic enough to plan a main course that takes hours to prepare, definitely do an easy dessert.

Keep a recipe file. Whether it's a box of index cards or a loose-leaf binder, an organized file will make it easier to skim through recipes for menu suggestions. Jot down the preparation time. This will help you budget time when planning your next party.

Pretested recipes are a must. Guests should not be made to feel like laboratory animals. No matter how reputable your cookbook may be, try out the recipes first. Note some suggestions on your recipe cards like, "bake an extra five minutes" or "add more salt."

Pretest kitchen equipment, too. If you borrow a neighbor's coffeepot, try it out before the party. The second time you use it, you'll not only measure the right amount of coffee to make a perfect pot, you'll know exactly how long the coffee takes to brew.

Timing is very important. Establish a workable timetable for your oven as well as for yourself. Demanding cooking schedules can wear you out unnecessarily. Synchronize the cooking agenda. If you have only one oven and want to serve two dishes simultaneously, don't plan dishes that require two different cooking temperatures. Popovers and soufflés may be tempting, but together they might be too much for your nerves as well as your oven to handle. Trying to keep a classic hollandaise sauce from curdling is difficult to do when you're attempting to carve a roast at the same time. So plan a menu that doesn't require too much precision and simultaneous cooking.

In addition, if you serve the food over several courses, you will lighten your work load because you won't have so much to do at the same time. For example, Antoinette complained, "I had to ready four dishes for the main course and this required a lot of last-minute synchronization." Her solution— she served the salad as a separate course. Depending on your preference serve the salad either *before* or *after* the main course. (By the way, lettuce leaves can be washed, cut and stored in a plastic bag or tightly wrapped bowl in the refrigerator. Just before serving, simply add the dressing and toss.)

Make the service of foods as easy as possible for yourself.

Take a mental inventory of your dinnerware, serving bowls and platters. Plan a menu that is suitable to your supply of equipment. You can't serve ramekins of crabmeat if you don't have ramekins. Knowing beforehand which foods will be presented on which serving dishes will facilitate service.

What is easy for some is difficult for others. Plan a menu that is easy for *you* to cook and serve.

❦ *Appropriateness*

Plan a menu that is appropriate for the party. An "anything goes" attitude usually won't work.

Utilize recipes that are suitable to the theme and type of party planned. Serving hot dogs and corn-on-the-cob at a black-tie dinner and *coquilles St. Jacques* at a children's birthday party will not establish your reputation as an astute host. Rather, set a specific theme and build upon it. Plan a seafood dinner with all the delicacies of the ocean or a "Gone With The Wind" party with southern fried chicken and mint julep cocktails.

Prepare a menu that's in keeping with the season. This will please your pocket as well as your guests. Don't wear yourself out trying to find fresh strawberries in January or fresh pumpkins in July. Serve fresh green salads in summer and hot hearty soups in winter.

America is a melting pot and one school of thought is to prepare Italian food for people of Italian background, Greek food for Greeks, French food for French, and so on. I disagree. Your guests may often be experts in preparing and tasting dishes of their national origins and may easily detect flaws in the recipes. It's better to prepare something different. Besides, they might enjoy the change of pace.

Cook to please your guests. It's worthwhile to prepare a time-consuming dish for certain people, but not for those who won't appreciate it. Some guests will notice your efforts when you make veal Cordon Bleu, while others will be quite satisfied with broiled steak and a baked potato. Be discerning. Know your guests' preferences. One embarrassed host took two hours to prepare a magnificent frozen Grand Marnier soufflé only to learn at the party that the guest of honor was a teetotaler.

Coordinate the courses at your dinner party. Meatballs and spaghetti are fine served with antipasto but not with chow mein. One dish should complement the next. Certain foods go well with one another—cranberry sauce with turkey, baked beans with hot dogs, lemon flavoring with fish dishes. But then, a twist of the usual might be a pleasant surprise. Try a walnut instead of a pecan pie or a pineapple instead of an orange glaze sauce for roast duckling.

If your menu is inappropriate and poorly coordinated, it will detract from your party. If it is appropriate and well planned, it can only enhance the festivities.

ℰ *Balance*

Bring harmony to your menu by providing a nutritionally balanced meal that has an interesting blend of flavors, consistency, weight and color.

A nutritionally balanced meal is essential. Include at least one dish from each of the basic categories: meat, poultry or fish, vegetable, and starch. Use the best quality food your pocketbook can afford and use the freshest foods possible.

Be aware of the consistency of each dish. Offer an assortment of textures. Prepare some foods that are creamy and others that are plain; some that are smooth and others that are crisp and crunchy. Cream of potato soup, creamy shrimp Newburg, and Boston cream pie won't do. A pleasant variety of textures will add personality to your menu.

Prepare a medley of flavors. Did you ever go to a party where every dish was flavored with wine. The soup, the meat, the dessert, and guess what the beverage was. Some cooks get carried away with their favorite seasoning. It's best to have a diversity of flavors from bland to spicy and tart to sweet.

Along the same lines, one dish should not foreshadow another. I once went to a dinner party where cheese was the overpowering ingredient. It was served as an hors d'oeuvre, there was a cheese sauce on the vegetables and cheesecake was the dessert!

Plan a balance of hot and cold dishes. This will make advance preparation easy because cold dishes can usually be done ahead of time. It will also make serving easier. An appropriate menu might consist of three hot and three cold dishes. For example, a chilled fruit cup; a cold salad; a hot main course consisting of a meat, vegetable, and a starch; and a cold dessert.

A menu should have a delicate balance of lightness and heaviness. Preferably serve the lighter foods first and build up to the heavier ones. Wines should be served in the same way. A rich menu that includes chicken tetrazzini, a rice dish, and stuffed eggplant might be too much for some guests to handle. If you decide to serve a heavy main course, plan a lighter first course.

Coordinate the color of foods on the dish. Food must first appeal to the eye before it appeals to the taste. How boring to serve only white foods. You may have scrumptious recipes for potatoes, cauliflower and chicken, but if you serve them together, they will look dull. Have fun when you are coloring your plates. My favorite is to prepare a green, red, and white Italian menu. Pimentos and mushrooms for the first course, boneless breast of chicken Parmesan, *fettuccine Alfredo*, and broccoli for the main course, followed by spinach salad and ending with zabaglione and strawberries for dessert.

Accessorize your foods with garnishes. A sprig of parsley or a slice of lemon sometimes adds just the right dash of color. Be sure your foods look as delectable as they taste.

One of the greatest inventions in the field of palate-pleasing delights is a hot fudge sundae. It is an excellent example of combining flavor, consistency, weight and color. The hotness of the fudge balances the coldness of the ice cream, the creaminess of the sauce balances the crunchiness of the nuts, the lightness of the whipped cream balances the heaviness of the ice cream, and the chocolate balances the vanilla in color and in flavor. It may not be nutritionally balanced, but a hot fudge sundae sure pleases the eye and comes close to perfection.

𝒬4

It's Not Only
What But How

𝒬 It's All In The Presentation

Present the food and drinks with a flair. It is not only what
you do and serve, but it is *how* you do it. *How* you serve the
food, *how* you offer the drinks, *how* you treat the guests and
how you handle yourself. That's what gets results. Your surroundings may be humble, your decorations unpretentious,
and your food simple, but they can all emerge dazzling, if you
know the "how" of entertaining.

Learn the "how" of hospitality. Open your arms as you open
your home. Put yourself in your guests' place. Feel their feelings. From the minute friends arrive at your home, let them
feel welcome and comfortable. Make them feel at ease by providing an introduction that provokes conversation with other
guests. When you serve drinks, offer suggestions so guests
don't feel embarrassed to ask for something you might not
have. Try to anticipate any awkward or embarrassing moments, and think beforehand how you will handle them. Make
your guests feel pampered and special in your home.

Even when someone asks for a glass of water you can serve
it with style. Water is water, you say. Not so. Pour it into a
tall, thin glass, chilled with lots of ice cubes. Present it on a

silver tray accompanied by a lace-trimmed napkin. Now *that's* a glass of water.

🎗 Smooth Arrivals

Put out the welcome mat before your guests arrive at the door. In the evening the outside lights as well as the party room lights should be on; the house numbers visible. Keep the driveway clear of toys and tools. In the winter, pave a clear path through the snow and don't forget to close the garage doors. If you live in an apartment building, notify the door-man that you are expecting a crowd. Or, if you have a buzzer system, make sure that it's in working order and that your name is clearly marked in its proper place.

Be ready at least fifteen minutes before the guests are sup-posed to arrive. By doing this you will always be prepared for early arrivers. Otherwise, the few extra minutes can be used for last-minute preparations, or simply, for relaxing. Guests feel uncomfortable when they arrive on time for a party and greet the hostess rushing downstairs from the bedroom fasten-ing her necklace and the host knotting his necktie. So, if your guests are courteous enough to be on time, you should be too.

It should not be expected nor considered fashionable for guests to arrive ten to fifteen minutes late although the world seems to be running ten minutes late nowadays. What hap-pened to the days when seven o'clock meant seven o'clock not 7:10 or 7:15? (Were there ever those days?) Some *guests* think it is polite to be ten minutes late. And some *hosts* expect guests to be ten minutes late. I have one friend who means seven o'clock when she says, "Cocktails will be served at 7:00." If I arrive at 7:12, she tells me in no uncertain terms that I am twelve minutes late. I have another friend who expects me to arrive at 7:30 when she invites me for dinner at 7:00. The problem is knowing *who* means *what*. Don't play games with time. Seven o'clock should mean seven o'clock. Hosts and guests should be on time.

Greet your guests personally at the door. They deserve this attention no matter how busy you are in the kitchen when they arrive. If you have taken care of all of the necessary preparations in advance, the chores should be minimal. You should be ready and relaxed to meet your guests. Definitely plan to attend your own party right from the start.

Decide before the guests arrive what you will do with their coats. If you have a guest coat closet, have extra hangers ready. It's easier to hang coats when you don't have to fumble for space in an overcrowded closet. If you live in a small apartment and are having a large party, make arrangements to have a coat rack in the hallway. Smooth arrivals allow you and your guests to get on with the party.

❧ "I'd like you to meet . . ."

Include a short fact about each person when introducing your guests to each other. Adding a brief anecdote or mentioning a person's hobby can pave the way to easier conversation. "Donna, I'd like you to meet Ray, who just spent two weeks vacationing in California. Ray, this is Donna. She used to live there."

Tell your relationship to the person you are introducing. "This is an old school friend of mine," "This is my tennis partner," or "This is my husband's coworker." This does not mean that you should label or classify each individual. Such stereotyping can be rude and more uncomfortable than no comment at all.

Use a common denominator that you already know interests both parties. "Marie, I'd like you to meet Ann. She, like you, is very interested in French cooking." Or, "David, this is Michael. He is taking a wine appreciation course and shares your interest in the subject." Don't wait for the middle of the party for your friends to discover, "Gee, it's a small world." Simply think of your guests' interests or background and, if possible, plan ahead for your party introductions.

After six or eight guests have arrived and have been introduced, it is not necessary to call a halt to all conversation upon the arrival of other guests. You've worked hard to get those conversations going, so don't stop them now. Introduce the newly arriving guests to a few people but not to everyone in the room. For a large party, after a few introductions, suggest that the guests introduce themselves. Try to get the newcomers talking in new groups.

I went to a party where there were twenty-eight guests present. When the twentieth-ninth and thirtieth persons arrived, the host interrupted all conversation, introduced the two new people, and proceeded clockwise around the room naming each guest. Maybe he was exercising a newly learned technique of name memorization, but, unfortunately, it disrupted all other conversation.

Make introductions meaningful. Provoke conversations and your guests will feel at ease.

❦ A Flowing Conversation

Keep the conversation going and flowing, naturally and comfortably. All of the guests may not know one another, but it is up to you to know your guests. A lull in the conversation can be awkward. To avoid these breaks, prepare a mental list of one or two questions for each guest. For example, "Joan, how did you enjoy the new restaurant you tried last week?" or "How is the patio you are building coming along, Bob?" Make sure the answer requires more than a "yes" or "no." When the lull comes, all you have to do is to call upon your mental list of questions and the conversation will flow once again. The guests never need to know that you had these thoughts prepared in advance.

Greet each guest at the door, but don't leave it at that. No matter how large the party is, speak to each guest individually, even if it is just for a few moments. And when you are with a guest, talk to that person as if he or she were the only person in the room. Don't wave to others in the middle of a conversation or look out of the corner of your eye to see who's coming in and going out. Be interested in each guest; make everyone you speak to feel special.

Include everyone in the conversation. It is your duty to keep a watchful eye for the wallflower. Don't attract attention to the shy guest, but make an inconspicuous attempt to introduce the person to someone else. Even if you'd rather spend the entire evening talking to the fascinating and articulate person on your right, turn to the silent one on your left and try to include him or her in the conversation, too.

Let your guests entertain each other. All you have to do is get the conversation started between two guests and they'll do the rest. And remember what I suggested in the section on introductions—mention something each guest might enjoy discussing. The mark of a proficient host or hostess is one who keeps the conversation flowing and does it effortlessly.

✌ *"What would you like to drink?"*

Recognize the hesitant feeling a shy guest may have when asked what he or she would like to drink. In fact, with any guest it's gracious to offer some suggestions. Instead of pursuing the usual ritualistic dialogue—"What do you want to drink?"—"Well, what do you have?"—"Whatever you want," —which ultimately leaves no one the wiser, make some specific suggestions. "Would you like a drink? We have chilled white wine, beer, bloody marys, or would you prefer Scotch?" You need not give a complete inventory of your liquor cabinet. The intent is merely to make some suggestions so that your guest will feel at ease.

If you don't have a bartender (and how many of us do?), then decide in advance who will make the cocktails. Guests feel uneasy when hosts bicker over the job, "I made the last round of drinks, it's your turn now, dear!" Better yet, set up a self-service bar. Make the first drink for your guests and encourage them to help themselves thereafter.

Decorate the drinks with garnishes such as lemons, limes and olives. They enhance the appeal of the drink, are relatively inexpensive and require a minimum amount of preparation. Try a celery stick stirrer for a bloody mary or sugar on the rim of a frozen daiquiri. Alan, a creative host, tints ice cubes with cherry juice for an unusual touch in some of his vodka drinks.

In addition to garnishes, remember it's *how* you serve the

drinks that counts. A sensational glass, such as an oversized, long-stemmed wine glass, will make any drink inviting. If the glass is fun to drink out of, the cocktail tastes delicious. And drinking out of a terrific glass makes guests feel special, too.

Richard offered wine to his guests; all accepted, but one. However, the guest changed her mind when she saw how the wine was presented. The bowl of each elegant crystal goblet measured five inches in diameter. "Oh that looks so good. I think I *will* have some," she said.

"Would you like some hors d'oeuvres?"

Make the food look appealing, too. Appearance is so important. But, of course, it should never be at the expense of taste. Arrange your hors d'oeuvres colorfully and creatively. Let your dishes be a feast for the eyes to devour. Even the most ordinary snacks can look fantastic on a pedestal dish, decorative tray or attractive platter.

Go lightly on the hors d'oeuvres at a dinner party. Emphasize the beauty rather than the bounty. Keep in mind that the focal point of the party is the meal you have thoughtfully prepared. Rather than have a variety of premeal goodies that rivals the number of flavors at your favorite ice cream parlor, put the extra effort into garnishing the limited number of hors d'oeuvres you choose to serve. Go to town with parsley, pimentos, lemon slices and anything else you can think of for decoration.

For a cocktail party, think of how you will present each dish attractively. Whether you're offering hot and cold hors d'oeuvres, dips or canapés, serve food with imagination and style.

Remember, it's *how* you serve that counts. Try serving an ordinary dip in a natural bread bowl. Use a round, unsliced loaf of pumpernickel bread. Cut off the top. Hollow out the bread and put the dip into the shell. Cube the inside bread and use it for dipping. Any dip becomes impressive when it is cleverly served.

Place the food in a convenient spot so your guests can feel

comfortable helping themselves. It is not sensible to place a cheese platter off in a corner of the room if all the guests are comfortably centered around the fireplace and have to leave their places to have a bite. They feel as if everyone is looking at them. And, usually, everyone is!

When you bring out the hors d'oeuvres from the kitchen, assist some of your guests to the first helping. Cut the first piece of cheese, spread the first cracker; then tell them to help themselves. This puts guests at ease.

❧ Unusual Serving Pieces

Be innovative in choosing your serving dishes. Use a tray, platter, or dish to hold something other than what was originally intended. It's daring and it's fun.

If you have a beautiful champagne bucket but serve champagne infrequently, don't let it just sit in the closet. Line it with a colorful cloth napkin and serve pretzel sticks in it. Serve potato chips in a very large brandy snifter. Serve cookies, pies, or even cheese and crackers on a pedestal cake plate. Serve a wedge of cheese on an attractive square of ceramic tile.

Before you serve food and snacks or set your dinner or buffet table, take a serious inventory of your china closet. Look in the attic for those never-used house or wedding gifts and start serving creatively. The trick is to be imaginative with the serving pieces you already have. Were you given an unusual shaped pitcher as a gift? Put some cut flowers in it to perk up the entrance foyer.

A nut dish for nuts? A relish dish for relish? A vegetable dish for vegetables? How boring. Use your imagination; be slightly bizarre. Your guests will notice and admire the unique style that makes you *you*.

❦ Offering Seconds

Prepare an ample amount of food. You can't offer seconds if you don't have enough. And, be aware of *how* you offer the seconds.

The normal request, "Would anyone like some more?" will sometimes be sufficient. However, if you sense a shy guest needs a little persuasion, say to that person, "The best compliment to the chef (which is me) is a guest who has seconds." Usually, this will be enough for your friend to say, "Well, in that case, I *will* have another, please." On the other hand, don't be too forceful, or even worse, a nag about seconds. There's nothing more annoying than having food forced upon you when you really feel that you've had enough. I know grandmothers have license to say, "Eat, eat, eat," but a host's constant coaxing can make a guest feel uncomfortable.

❦ Delectable Desserts

Serve desserts with pizzazz! To many guests, this is the most important course. Whether you are serving dessert formally at a sit-down dinner for business associates, informally at a buffet for the neighbors, or while sitting around the cocktail table in the living room with close friends, do it with panache. Setting up the cake and coffee in the kitchen and passing the word around the party just doesn't make it. Serve in the kitchen if you must, but let it be spectacular.

At a farewell luncheon for a friend who was moving to Florida, Cynthia made a cake in the shape of a state. She wrote "Tampa" on a stemmed banner and strategically placed it on the cake. She inscribed the words "au revoir and farewell" in colorful icing. The hostess's creativity turned an ordinary iced cake into a real delight.

Any dessert, attractively presented, adds flavor to the party before it is even tasted. Pedestal dishes with doilies add zip and zest to the appearance of cookies, cakes and pies. Chocolate pudding or ice cream will always taste better served in a stemmed champagne glass instead of a paper cup. If you're really daring, plan a flaming dessert as a finale and let it make a grand entrance.

Use glasses, cups and mugs that are fun to drink from. Irish coffee glasses are marvelous for espresso, *cappuccino*, and unusual teas as well. And instead of using the everyday coffeepot, put in the extra effort to polish up the silver coffee service. Guests will recognize and appreciate the flair you display when serving desserts.

❧ *And Finally, Flexibility*

Don your gown of flexibility and wear it for the entire evening. It's an outfit that will get you many compliments if your guests are perceptive.

You've done as much in advance for your party as you could. The shopping, cooking and cleaning are finished. The table is set. You are feeling relaxed and confident as your first guests arrive. Now, be flexible.

Maintain your poise if something unusual happens. Don't be too unnerved if a guest is late, arrives with an unexpected friend or comes in the back door. Handle it with diplomacy. If you drop a platter of hors d'oeuvres or spill a whole bottle of wine, keep calm. Clean it up quickly and forget about it. These tragedies sometimes do happen. Don't let them ruin your party. If the main course burns or you forget to buy milk for the coffee, be honest with your guests. Tell them. Laugh about it. Then use your ingenuity with what you have left or run out to the corner grocery store. Drinks will spill and glasses will break, but the guests will remember long after the party how well you "picked up the pieces."

While having cocktails at a party, a careless guest left a lit cigarette in an ashtray on the couch. The cigarette rolled out and embedded itself in the cushions. Later, when the guests were enjoying dinner, they smelled smoke. The couch was smoldering and, obviously, too late for salvation. The quick-thinking host, Robert, asked the guests for assistance. They carried the sofa outdoors. Robert even joked about not having marshmallows for a campfire. With a fast spray of the lawn hose the fire was out. Although he must have been terribly upset, he realized there was nothing he could do. He was quick in his actions, prevented a more serious problem, and laughed along with his guests over a situation that was unfortunate, but which, nevertheless, did happen.

Alter your plans if necessary. If some guests are late or others linger over cocktails, dinner may have to be delayed a few minutes. If you've planned to serve after-dinner drinks on the patio but the guests seem to be content at the dining room table, stay there. Flexibility will let you enjoy your own party, make your guests feel at ease, and turn any crisis into a mere mishap.

ℰ5

Table Settings:
The Stage For The Party

ℰ Setting The Stage

Set the stage for your party by setting a table that reflects both your personality and the theme of the party. Intensify the feeling of the party with an attractive table setting. Create an elegant mood with monogrammed napkins, fine china, and silver. If your style is more informal, add character to a cozy atmosphere with a gingham tablecloth and pottery plates and mugs. For a summer garden party, use lots of fresh flowers on the table to heighten the spirit of gaiety. And for a youthful appearance at a children's party, decorate the table with candy-striped napkins and a polka-dotted tablecloth in bold, striking colors.

Carmel, an exceptional hostess, outdid herserlf one evening at a seafood dinner party. The tablecloth and napkins were in shades of coral, green, and white. The centerpiece was a clear bowl filled with a variety of seashells in water; a gardenia floated on top. On either side of the centerpiece were two conch shells holding tapered candles. Seashells in assorted shapes and sizes were arranged attractively on the table as well as being affixed to the place cards. The first course, mixed seafood au gratin, was served on individual scallop shells. The dishes were ordinary white and the flatware was nothing outstanding. Yet, with a minimum of cost and a maximum of ingenuity, Carmel set a noteworthy table with the aura of the sea.

There are two major contributors to a well-groomed table—color and uniformity. Color plays a central role. Bring it out in the linens, dishes, or centerpiece. Color adds vitality and zest to the whole table. Don't worry about matching the color of your table setting with the color of the room; that's too limiting. If the table is set attractively, all eyes will focus on it rather than on the colors in the wallpaper.

Uniformity is as important as color. Pay attention to details. Establish a sense of continuity when placing the napkins, flatware, and dishes on the table.

If you adhere to the rules of table-setting etiquette, you will bring harmony and consistency to your table. Forks are placed to the left of the plate, except seafood forks, which belong on the right of the plate next to the knives and spoons. Knife blades should be turned towards the plate. Water and wine glasses are placed in the upper righthand corner of the place setting, above the knife and spoons. Butter plates are quietly fading from the table for a very practical reason—there's just not enough room. Nevertheless, when they are used, they are placed in the upper lefthand corner of the table setting, above the forks.

Be sure all the accessories are consistent with the theme. Have a rhyme to your mixing and matching. Forget the breakable heirloom china at a patio party and a hand-embroidered cloth at a children's party. Don't mix plastic glassware with fine china. There are appropriate but separate times for all.

Because your party is a special occasion that deserves a special setting, invest your talents in a unique table creation that will be a festive backdrop for the whole party.

❧ Assembling The Cast

Assemble your table accouterments with an eye towards practicality and versatility. Buy dishes that can be cleaned in the dishwasher—ones that can play a number of roles from formal to carefree. Purchase glasses that are multipurpose. Use no-iron napkins and table coverings. You don't have to own four different sets of dishes and glasses. With creativity and ingenuity you can style a table that is suitable for any occasion.

Change the accessories and change the mood. Different table linens, napkin rings, place card holders, and centerpieces can create an ambience that's just right for your party.

There is no precise number of dishes that are a must in every breakfront. If you are just starting out and are assembling your table accessories, consider the type of entertaining you will do most. Service for twelve would be needless if you feel overwhelmed with ten guests already. If you like to entertain formally and appreciate the beauty of fine china, then by all means start collecting your set. If you have a lovely backyard and enjoy outdoor entertaining, it might be worthwhile to invest in a picnic table or a set of attractive unbreakable dishes. However, if you live in a small apartment with a two-by-four terrace, you won't need the picnic table. Don't buy on impulse. Think of how often and in how many ways you will use an item and then consider purchasing it.

Decide which method of service would be best for a particular party. When setting the table for a sit-down dinner consider the comfort of the guests. Don't stuff bodies around a table. Seat as many people as is comfortably possible. When serving buffet style remember to consider the patterns of traffic flow.

Your table setting is a reflection of your self. While most guests are generally unaware of all the effort you put into the party's preparation, one of the first things they are likely to notice about your party is the table. People notice two kinds of tables—the outstanding ones that are thoughtfully and meticulously set and the abominable ones. A mediocre table draws little attention. But, then, who wants to set a mediocre table?

❧ *A Wardrobe Of Table Coverings*

Perk up the look of the dishes you purchased years ago by changing the table coverings. Changing the tablecloth is easier and less expensive than buying a whole new set of dishes. And today there's such an assortment of coverings from which to choose.

Purchase attractive placemats in solid colors or prints, lace or quilted to achieve the effect you desire. Use them on a bare table or over a cloth. Cloths, too, come in a potpourri of colors, designs, and floral patterns so that you can change the complexion of your table settings. A classic off-white lace cloth is distinctive, versatile, and practical. Change the color of the underliner for variety. Or top off a lace cloth, or any other cloth, with a runner. There are a number of runners available from solid or patterned wash-and-wears to laces and felts. Buy them or make your own. Runners look particularly attractive on tables set for a buffet.

My favorite way to decorate the table is with ribbons. For a luxurious effect at Christmas, use 1½ inch-wide red velvet ribbon crisscrossed on top of white cloth. For a summer buffet, try thin strips of dotted swiss or floral cloth ribbon and stream them across the table. Make matching bows with extra ribbon, and secure them to the handle of wicker baskets which hold flatware and napkins. At one dinner party, I used strips of lavender, pink, and white plaid ribbon. The ribbons extended from the center of the table to each person's place setting. The cloth was solid pink, but the combination of colors in the ribbon added the right amount of color and interest. Ribbon is an inexpensive item that can be changed from party to party, table setting to table setting, and still offer an eye-catching result.

Color is such an important part of every table setting. Establish a light carefree mood with pastel shades or a spectacular look with deep vivid colors. On a practical note, printed clothes are more functional because wine and food stains won't show as easily as on light solid colors. Sally uses a solid black cloth. Believe it or not, it's quite attractive. "My dishes," she says, "are off-white so the black cloth really shows them up. And I love it because the stains never show."

Thank goodness, the days of endless ironing are over. We live in a wash-and-wear generation and should take advantage of it. We can change our table linens as easily as we change our clothes. There's no reason to always have the same "look." Monotony is out—diversity is in.

ℰ Casting Your Dishes

Cast your dishes in a variety of roles by changing the table accessories. Dress up ordinary dishes with a lace tablecloth and silver candlesticks. Or give dishes a sporty look with deep-colored plaid napkins and wrought-iron napkin rings. Or combine two styles in an eclectic look. If it is done properly, it can be very attractive.

Don't feel restricted by your particular set of dishes. If your dishes are a multicolored floral pattern, choose one or two colors for your scheme. Bring them out in the centerpiece, the napkins, or the table covering. Develop another color scheme for another party. On the other hand, if your dishes are plain, all the options are yours. Enrich the table by adding lots of color in the other table appointments.

Everything doesn't have to match. Mix patterns but do it with a system. Use all the same dinner plates in a printed pattern and all the same soup bowls in a solid color. Or alternate each place setting with different colors. For an Independence Day party, set an all-red place setting, next to an all-blue place setting, followed by an all-white place setting and so on. Or use a medley of different dish patterns. Be sure each is different enough so that it's obvious that you are *not* trying to match all of them. Mix designs but even with that, establish harmony by using all china, all pottery, or all stoneware dishes. Anything goes, as long as there's a method.

Arrange the dishes neatly on the table. There should be balance and consistency. Table-setting etiquette is practical because it affords comfort to the guests and provides the orderliness that is so necessary on a table. Each place should be set in a uniform pattern.

✌ *The Direction Of Flatware*

Place the flatware neatly on the table. Eating utensils don't have to be sterling to be rich with charm. Whether your service is sterling, silverplate, or stainless steel, an orderly table is more noteworthy than the price of your forks and spoons.

For a dinner party, arrange the flatware in one of the two traditional positions. Either line up the bottom of the handles or the junctions of the handles evenly. (See illustration p. 56) Whichever position you choose, be sure each guest's place is the same. Dessert utensils are not included in a dinner table setting and are distributed with the service of dessert unless they are positioned on the table horizontally at the top of the dinner plate. In this case, the handle of the fork should be faced left and the handle of the spoon should be faced right. The uniformity of each place adds to the beauty of the table.

The menu determines the order of flatware. Guests will start eating with the utensils placed to the farthest outside position then work towards the plate. Here again, following the rules of table-setting etiquette is a practical idea. When you are setting a table if you are in doubt whether to put out a spoon or fork for a particular food, use this general guide. If the food is served on a flat dish, use a fork. If the food is served in a rounded dish or soup bowl, use a spoon.

A little habit that irks me is to see the forks placed on top of the napkin. Forks go on the left. Napkins do, too. But forks don't go on top of napkins. This is not one of those rules for rules' sake. There is a logical reason. When you arrive at the table, the first thing you usually do is place the napkin on your lap. If the forks are on top of the napkin, the order of the setting will be upset, not to mention the needless rattle of clanging forks. Unfortunately, even the most knowledgeable hosts still make this mistake.

For a buffet, be practical about the arrangement of flatware.

Optional placement of flatware: above, line up the junctions of the handles; below, line up the bottom of the handles.

For your guests' convenience and to add a decorative touch, wrap the eating utensils in a colorful napkin and secure them with ribbon tied into a tiny bow. Arrange them symmetrically on the table. The guests can pick up their little bundles with one motion. For a space-saving idea at an outdoor picnic, place the flatware in a clean terra cotta flowerpot or wicker basket. Use anything attractive rather than those cheap styrofoam cups as containers.

❦ *Standing Ovation Glassware*

Delight your guests by using glasses that are really fun to drink from. A magnificent glass will make most any drink appealing. My favorite "standing ovation" glasses are large-bowled, long-stemmed crystal goblets. The bowls are four inches in diameter and they hold fourteen ounces. (Fill them only one-

14 oz. multipurpose glass; 8 oz. versatile tulip-shape glass; slender flute.

third to one-half.) They are multipurpose glasses that can be used for fruit salads, desserts, and chilled summer soups as well as for wine. If your taste is not so grandiose, a versatile tulip-shape stemmed glass that holds at least eight or ten ounces can be used for red or white wine or even champagne.

Traditionally, there is a distinction between red and white wine glasses. What was a "must" on any well-set table twenty years ago, is not an absolute today. Hosts should, of course, still offer separate glasses when serving both red and white wine; however, the traditional shapes are no longer insisted upon except by the most discriminating connoisseurs.

On the other hand, a specific shape *is* preferred today for champagne: the slender flute. The longer bowl allows the drinker to fully appreciate the lively effervescence. What, you might ask, are you supposed to do if you have a set of those shallow champagne glasses that are now out-of-date. Serve desserts or intermezzo (p. 000) in them; fill them with nuts or after-dinner mints. Or, you can simply refuse to "go along with the crowd" and use your shallow champagne glasses for champagne. Either way, do what pleases *you* most.

Like dishes, all glasses set on a dinner table do not have to match. Mix patterns and designs but do it with continuity. Use all the same wine glasses from one set and all the same water glasses from another. Be sure the glasses are clean and dust-free before you put them on the table.

For large cocktail or buffet parties, many liquor stores will supply the glasses free of charge if you purchase the liquor from them. If you borrow the store's glasses, you won't have to use plastic glasses. There are some parties, like outdoor picnics, when it is fitting to use plastic glasses, but most guests prefer "real" glasses to plastic ones. Sure you can get away with using plastic throwaways, but a real glass is more comfortable to drink from.

❦ The Supporting Role Of Napkins

Dress your table with pretty napkins. Like table coverings, there's a tremendous selection of napkins available. Your napkins do not have to be exactly the same print or color as the tablecloth or placemats.

For a dinner, place your napkins either on the service plate or to the left of the forks. Fold your napkins in any one of several ways. In addition to the usual rectangle and triangle, many hosts are folding napkins in the shape of fans, flowers, cones, and other distinctive shapes.

You don't have to limit yourself to the conventional. While I don't particularly like to see napkins stuffed in glasses and flapping in the air like flags at the U.N., I do try to be creative with each table setting. For an informal buffet, I'd display the napkins in a wicker basket or clean flower pot, and, for a more formal buffet, I'd use a silver or crystal wine cooler as a container.

Another option is to use decorative napkin rings. Choose from a variety of clear, colored, silver, straw, lucite, and enamel ones. There are napkin rings in the shape of flowers and seashells. Don't limit yourself to the store-bought ones alone. Wrap a thin, colored ribbon around the napkin, and tie it in a tiny bow. The ribbon can coordinate with your color scheme and match the ribbon you use as a runner. For a baby shower, secure each napkin with a diaper pin. Use your imagination for every party.

Make your own napkins, too. From a remnant piece of fabric, use pinking shears to make cloth napkins for a barbecue or pool party. In the long run it may be less expensive than buying paper napkins.

Napkins, besides being functional, are decorative. They help carry out your color scheme and establish the mood of the entire setting, along with the dishes, glassware and other accessories. Hand-embroidered white linen napkins add an elegant touch to a formal affair, while red-and-white check napkins conjure up the atmosphere of a French bistro. To achieve a total effect, be sure the napkins you choose are consistent with the other table appointments.

℘ An Encore Of Extras and Accents

Take the time to incorporate your most attractive serving pieces into your table setting and food presentation. One or two wine bottles on the table are acceptable, but rather than display a gallon jug, use a wine decanter or a pitcher. Even water is more appealing when poured from a crystal pitcher. A milk container, large soda bottles, and beer cans will detract from the table you so conscientiously set. One plastic margarine container can steal the show from the most exquisite china and silver. Spread the margarine into a small dish or bowl or use stick margarine.

Renée and Joe told me about an unusual dinner party they attended. The table was tastefully set with fine china, crystal, and sterling. The centerpiece, an impressive fresh flower arrangement, was surrounded by ornate silver candlesticks. However, all these embellishments could not compensate for the cardboard bucket of take-out chicken that was being passed around the table. It was so inappropriate, it was funny. The least the host could have done was to put the chicken in another dish.

A practical but decorative asset is oven-to-table cookware. Instead of taking the time to transfer food to a platter, you can bring it to the table immediately. This ovenware comes in all different sizes from casserole to soufflé dishes and has a variety of patterns from which to choose. Some are elegant enough to grace a formal table.

Your own tasteful extras and accents will give personality to your table. Use individual salt cellars, pewter service dishes, an antique set of demitasse cups, or whatever pièce de résistance is your "cup of tea."

❦ Center Stage With Centerpieces

Highlight your table setting with an eye-catching centerpiece. Of all the accessories, it plays the major role in bringing color and decoration to a table. Here, again, is your chance to be as creative and innovative as you wish.

Traditionally, fresh flowers are most often used. They can be formally arranged in an attractive container or casually clustered in a small vase. The trend today seems to be away from formal arrangements. Some people see them as stiff and funereal, but I prefer to think of them as classics that are always in vogue. A formal arrangment does not have to be costly or even arranged by a florist. Make your own design. Buy some inexpensive flowers or use whatever you have available in your garden—ivy, rhododendron, dogwood, or holly. To hold the stems in place, use an oasis: a soft, spongy substance that you saturate with water.

For a sensational impact, arrange miniature containers of flowers for each place setting. Model them on the main centerpiece. For containers, I often use the plastic tops of aerosol spray cans. I place the oasis inside and cover the outside with decorative foil; they add a breath of charm to any table.

An edible centerpiece is practical as well as popular. It can be as simple as a bowl of colorful vegetables and mixed fruit like apples, radishes, lemons, cauliflower, plums, peppers, and oranges. Or it can be as dazzling as bouquets of sculptured vegetables and wreaths of fruits and nuts. You'll probably find your guests nibbling at the centerpiece.

Plastic fruit and crystal beaded vegetables are out of style.

Inanimate objects are currently popular. Baskets, bottles and bowls in a variety of shapes and sizes make attractive displays. Dried and silk flower arrangements are practical because they can be used over and over again. Ice sculptures are in the avant-garde of centerpieces. They were originally used on buffet tables in posh restaurants. Now some enterprising people are making their own at home. Department stores are selling ice molds in the shapes of flowers, animals, fish and Christmas trees.

Centerpieces can develop holiday themes. Use a cornucopia filled with fresh fruits, nuts, and gourds on a Thanksgiving Day table. For Halloween, use a pumpkin with colorful ribbon streaming from the stem and place it on a plate covered with crimson leaves. Christmas is a wonderful season for all kinds of handmade goodies that can be arranged as centerpieces— pine cone wreaths, fabric-made trees, baskets filled with Christmas tree balls, handmade angels, candles, and artificial snowmen.

Whatever your centerpiece creation, be sure that its size is moderate and that its height remains below eye level. Monstrosities that overpower the table and huge flower arrangements done up in elaborate containers make it difficult for the guests to see and talk to one another. Usually, in such cases, one frustrated but courageous guest will reach out and remove the obstruction while the others silently applaud.

The centerpiece is the focal point of the table and should remain in the limelight for the entire evening. If its size is appropriate, there's no reason for you or the guests to take it away. Once the food is served, many hosts think they have to remove the centerpiece to make room for platters and bowls of food. I prefer to set up a server or sideboard to hold the serving dishes and leave the centerpiece highlighted on the table where it belongs.

ℰ Candlelight

Create an enchanting atmosphere in the evening with candlelight. Candles, today, come in a charming variety of shapes and sizes. Most formal tables will have tapers on either side of the centerpiece, but tradition does not have to limit their placement. Cluster a group of candles around the center of the table or set off your place settings by putting a votive candle at the head of each plate. On a long table, position a row of candlesticks in graduated sizes along the table. Instead of the usual tapers, use the new "floating candles" which are actually wicks inserted into plastic discs that float on water—elegant as a centerpiece in a decorative bowl or in attractive stemmed glasses. Tint the water with food coloring to match your color scheme.

A room's lighting establishes ambience. If you are going to use candlelight, have a dimmer switch attached to your ceiling fixture. It's an inexpensive device that's well worth the investment.

Whether candles are the focal point of your table, the accessories, or the little extras at each place setting, they always contribute a touch of romance.

6

It's The Little Things

The Finishing Touches

Destine your party for success. It's the little things that really count. Your combination of individual touches can create a masterpiece of a party that is bound to have a dynamic effect.

A party can be *just* a party—people, food, and drink. Don't settle for the usual. Set your party apart from everyone else's. No, not necessarily with lavish food and expensive decorations. Make the evening unique because of *your* little finishing touches.

Start with the invitations. Make them fun. Then use your creativity in planning all the details—the menu, the decorations, and the table setting—right down to the after-dinner mints. It's the thoughtful little extras that add a personal touch to your party.

I went to a party in honor of a woman named Rosa. The hostess personalized the party to the finest detail. She arranged a bouquet of roses from her garden in the entrance foyer and roses in the centerpiece. She put a long-stemmed rose at each place setting and folded the napkins in the shape of a flower. She attached a tiny picture of a rose to each place card and used a menu card bordered with roses. Rosa (and everyone else) loved it!

Be imaginative and be thoughtful. Plan to please your guests. Follow your creative impulses; put your mind in a party mood and let the inspirations flow.

❦ Inviting Invitations

Begin the party's fun with the invitations. Don't wait for the day of the party. Invitations set the mood.

Enclose a "surprise" in the envelope: for an autumn party —a crimson leaf, for a ski party—a paper cut-out snowflake, for a seafood dinner—a seashell, for a baby shower—a diaper pin, and for a birthday party—a candle. Your guests will taste the flavor of your party and savor what's to come.

Write a poem, song or limerick, if you are so inclined. Send your invitation in the form of a secret code and let your friends enjoy deciphering the message. There's a little Sherlock Holmes in all of us. Send a crossword puzzle or anagram. If the invitation is fun, imagine what the party will be!

I knew a clever host who enclosed a small wooden spoon in a colorful envelope for a "share-the-cooking" party and another who sent a plastic champagne glass in a decorative box with a note inside saying, "To be filled at . . ."

Forget the fill-in-the-blank kind of invitation. Personally, I'm tired of getting the stereotypical New Year's Eve invitation which pictures a drunk, wearing top hat and tails, holding a champagne glass, leaning against the lamp post, inviting me to "come and make merry." I'd much rather receive a hand written note with a sprinkle of confetti tucked inside.

Use bold-colored stationery and write the invitation yourself. It doesn't take any more time than the fill-in-the-blank ones. How long does it actually take to write, "We're having a party on . . . at. . . . Please come." The personal touch is such an asset.

Paper is not the only medium, so don't limit yourself. Cut out some remnant fabric with pinking shears and write with a

Spring

Formal Dinner . . . pink underliner, white lace overcloth, and lavender plaid ribbons for added color . . . individual flower arrangements coordinated with centerpiece . . . reusable porcelain place cards . . . mints wrapped in lavender tulle and tied with matching ribbon at each place setting . . . written menu with spring bouquet on the card cover . . . silver napkin rings . . .

SAME TABLE—SAME DISHES FOUR DIFFERENT LOOKS

Summer
Seafood Buffet Lunch
. . . fish net draped over
solid blue cloth . . .
bright flowers in conch
shells arranged on
nautical wooden base
wrapped in rope . . .
condiments, lemon slices,
and salad served in real
shells . . . fresh shrimp
presented in a fish-
shaped platter . . .
flatware wrapped in floral
napkins tied with rope . . .

*Centerpiece Designs by
Doris Shannon,
Colonial House of Flowers,
Ridgewood, N.J.*

Autumn

Informal Dinner . . .
orange place mats on off-white tablecloth provide colorful background for off-white china . . . fresh pumpkin shells for soup bowls . . . large slow-burning candles in rustic wooden holders surrounded by autumn leaves as a centerpiece . . . orange napkins tied with gingham ribbon which is also used to perk up baskets filled with tiny pine cones . . . place cards with pumpkin stickers . . .

Winter

Christmas Eve Dinner
. . . red and green
patterned tablecloth . . .
matching napkins topped
with sprigs of holly . . .
colorful gifts at each place
setting with gift tags
serving as placecards . . .
mints wrapped in red
cellophane tied with
green ribbon . . . written
menu with Christmas
scenes on the card
cover . . . brandy
snifters, holding holly
which is secured at the
base in florists' clay, filled
with water and topped
with "floating candles"—
as a centerpiece . . .

felt-tipped pen, "Pool Party. . . ." Use the same fabric to make informal, matching napkins for your outdoor party.

The ideas are endless. All it takes is a little thought. Before the party, sit down and have a conversation with your imagination. Give it carte blanche and let it run wild!

❦ *Individualizing*

Add character to your table by personalizing for each guest. There are many ways to individualize. Place cards add a charming distinction and are practical, too. A handwritten menu contributes a touch of dignity. A gift at each place setting is thoughtful.

On the breakfast table, tiny cups of jelly or jam for each person make an ordinary morning meal momentous. Give personality to a breakfast tray for your overnight guest by including a copy of his or her favorite morning newspaper tied with a colorful ribbon. Individual coffee carafes and teapots are lovely if you are fortunate enough to own them.

At the dinner table, if you know who the smokers are, give each an ash tray and matches. Individual salt cellars and pepper mills are elegant. A votive candle at each place creates a romantic mood and the guests will admire them. You might hollow out an apple and set a three-inch household candle in it for each guest. The single lights will combine to embrace the whole table and your party will be a "glowing" success.

Think of serving food in individual portions or containers, as long as the work is not overwhelming for you. For a summer picnic, how about a box lunch for each guest, prepared in advance. Arrange a sandwich, piece of fruit, small sealed carafe of wine, plastic glass, and napkin in a shoe box. Wrap it as a gift with colorful, decorative paper. Store it in the refrigerator. Guests will find your idea original and fun and you will have far less work in serving at your party.

❦ *Place Cards*

Take advantage of the many benefits of place cards. Don't even consider them pretentious; they are practical, decorative and can be entertaining. Besides, people just *love* to see their names written or printed.

Place cards help alleviate the uncomfortable silence that occurs when people arrive at the table and do not know what is expected of them. Guests may wonder if they should next to, across from, or far away from their spouse. They wonder how they can avoid the bore who monopolized the conversation over cocktails. Amidst this confusion, one forceful guest often takes the initiative and pipes up with, "Let's sit man, woman, man, woman," and starts indicating, "Now you sit here, and you sit here."

When the seating is decided in advance, you have maximum control of the conversational arrangements. You don't run the risk of having some guest take over for you or of finding all the men congregated on one side of the table and all the women on the other. Believe it or not, this can happen! Place cards are the safe solution. And, if for no other reason, use place cards so no one will sit in *your* seat.

Be inventive in designing your place cards. Let the season create your ideas. Use a heart-shaped picture frame for Valentine's Day with your guest's name written on the paper insert. Write a name on each colored egg for an Easter party. Attach a green shamrock seal on a white place card for St. Patrick's Day. Have your children participate in the holiday spirit and make small Pilgrim hats out of construction paper for a Thanksgiv-for a Thanksgiving Day dinner.

I went to a party where the resourceful hostess pasted cut-out magazine pictures on the place cards. Each portrayed a guest's hobby, profession, or idiosyncrasy. No names were written, and the guests had to figure out where to set from the pictures. Another host used want ads from the classified section of the *New York Times* to identify each guest's place.

Plan a theme and carry it out with the place cards. On ordinary paper cards glue miniature bow ties, dried flowers, seashells, or fabric coordinated with your party decorations. If

you plan an ethnic meal, attach that country's flag to each card
—appropriate, and colorful as well.

All in all, give place cards the place they deserve.

℘ *Write The Menu*

Place a handwritten menu on the table simply because most
guests like to know what's coming. They enjoy the anticipation of delectable treats. If a mouth-watering main course is
planned, they might want to go lightly on the appetizer.
Friends shouldn't have to guess the menu by looking at the
flatware or the number of dishes set on the table or sideboard.
In fact, such guesswork might not occur to many people.

At a dinner party one time, Norman took a modest portion
of the first course so that he could enjoy the other courses—
only to discover that there were no other courses. Another
friend, Helen, told me of the reverse situation. She satisfied
herself with the dish that was served and later learned that
there were three more courses to follow. If you've ever found
yourself in either of these predicaments you need no further
convincing to display a written menu on the table.

Your menu doesn't have to be gold lettered or leather
bound; and there need not be one at each place setting. One
handwritten menu on your finest stationery is sufficient. Some
hosts use a blackboard or an easel. My favorite is to use a
greeting card with a blank insert. While I'm not in favor of
store-bought invitations, these store-bought cards are attractive and useful for menus. The covers are colorful and can be
coordinated with your table setting. They are easily obtained
in most card stores. Save the jacket and replace the insert with
a fresh piece of paper for the next party.

If you like, when writing out your menu, use the language
of the country in which the dish originated. It adds a certain
panache. Thus beef stew with wine becomes *boeuf bourguig-
non,* noodles with cream and Parmesan cheese becomes *fettuccine Alfredo,* and chicken with yellow rice becomes *arroz con
pollo.* If the title of your dish doesn't have enough *je ne sais*

quoi, then make one up. And for those recipes that are your own concoction, you might add *de la maison* (of the house) to the title.

❧ Creative Edibles

Liven up your cooking with a little ingenuity. You don't have to be a gourmet cook. If your fare is simple, simply make it fun to eat.

When serving fruit salad or melon balls use their natural containers as serving dishes. Attractively shape a cantaloupe half, a pineapple shell or an orange skin. Or use a whole, hollowed-out watermelon shell as a punch bowl for a large summer party. One host sculpted a whole watermelon into the shape of a shark, filled it with cut up fruit and used it as a centerpiece.

My favorite creative serving piece is to use a raw pumpkin shell as a soup tureen. I cut off the top of the pumpkin, hollow out the seeds and serve a vegetable soup in the shell. I sometimes use small pumpkins as individual soup bowls. The soup never leaks out, the rind doesn't get soggy, and the soup stays hot. It's a real crowd pleaser.

For shrimp cocktail serve the sauce in a hollowed-out lemon shell. On a fresh vegetable platter use a whole bell pepper to hold the carrot sticks. Tuna fish or chicken salad served at a luncheon makes a better impression when served in a fresh tomato shell.

Hosts today are being incredibly creative with butter sculptures. They make curls, shells and flowers. At one party the butter was cut in the shape of jungle animals with tiny cookie cutters. Ordinary butter becomes an out-of-the-ordinary delight through the efforts of creative party givers and their attention to detail.

By using your imagination to serve food, you, too, can add sparkle to otherwise ordinary dishes.

❦ *"A gift for me?"*

Make the unspoken statement to your friends, "You are special." A small gift at each place setting is the epitome of thoughtfulness. It does not have to be expensive or even store-bought. The simplicity of one fresh flower for each guest says it all. If you want to say it with an exclamation point, then make a miniature flower arrangement for each place setting that coordinates with the main centerpiece.

Seasonal gifts are apropos. For an elegant Christmas dinner party, place a tree ornament on each service dish for friends to take home and hang on their trees. For an autumn party, fill a tiny straw nut basket with miniature pine cones freshly picked from the tree in your yard. Individual potted shamrock plants are lovely for an all green and white St. Patrick's Day party. And a cute gift for each guest on Valentine's Day could be a chocolate heart wrapped in red foil. A colorfully decorated egg will be a treat at an Easter party.

For summer parties, I love fresh flowers galore. But if you want an elegant touch that will be everlasting, give each person a silk flower. They can take it home, put it in a bud vase and enjoy fond memories long after the day of your party. For the guests at your spring luncheon, how about a tiny nosegay made with cut fresh flowers from your garden inserted into a small white doily?

Edible gifts are very popular. If you intend to serve after-dinner mints, why not wrap two mints in colorful cellophane paper tied with a tiny ribbon for each guest? One at each setting adds a splash of color to your table and also gives it an individual touch. Wrap up nuts or cookies, too. Fortune cookies are always great fun after an oriental meal prepared in your wok.

These gift ideas are not limited to sit-down dinners. Decorate your buffet table by arranging the gifts around the centerpiece. When it's time to go home, give a memento to each guest. Your friends will appreciate your thoughtfulness.

❦ *Sprinkle Your Home With Thoughtfulness*

Anticipate your guests' needs and spoil them with the little things that count. Spread your thoughtfulness throughout your home.

Start with the bathroom. Set out your best hand towels. Have facial tissue and extra toilet tissue available. Be sure there is a *new* bar of soap, not one mud-stained from the children's day at play. Arrange fresh flowers in a vase or light a scented candle. In the medicine cabinet, keep a supply of safety pins and a mini sewing kit. These items will be handy for any emergency that might occur during the party. If a guest's stomach is feeling upset, he may be too embarrassed to tell you, especially when you and the cook are one and the same person. You'll emerge as a superhost if you leave some antacid tablets and aspirin on the bathroom shelf for such emergencies.

Carry your thoughtfulness into every party room with large bouquets of flowers. They don't have to be formal florist arrangements. Look in your own backyard and you'll be surprised at the wonderful array of natural greenery and color. Pick wild flowers along the road in the summertime. Believe it or not, ordinary weeds that grow wild in fields or along the highway look fantastic in a vase or basket at home. The fragrance of fresh flowers and accents of a colorful arrangement can perk up even the dullest rooms.

Your guests will feel pampered when you create a total effect with the little things that count.

ℰ7

Dinner Parties

ℰ In Defense Of Dinner Parties

Flatter your friends by inviting them to a dinner party at your home. There's no two ways about it—planning a dinner party is more time-consuming than merely serving dessert and coffee. However, a party that requires more effort from the hosts is bound to result in more appreciation from the guests. The more you put into a party, the more you get out of it. So, indulge your special friends with a special treat.

Hosts and guests approach dinner parties from different perspectives and, as a result, often maintain different attitudes. One guest said, "I feel complimented when someone invites me to dinner. I feel lost in the shuffle at large parties, but at a small dinner party I feel special."

On the other hand, a host said, "When I'm planning a party I want to do what's easiest for me. Isn't a cocktail or after-dinner party the easiest? A party where I just have to serve hors d'oeuvres and snacks seems to require less work than a whole dinner. Besides, I don't think I could handle a sit-down affair."

But, giving a dinner party does not have to be a dreaded experience like spring cleaning your house or final exams after a difficult school semester. With advance preparation and organization, almost any host or hostess can create a successful dinner party that guests will relish.

Richard, an accomplished host, whose dinner parties are a real treat, told me, "I prefer to give small, seated dinner parties. I can do most of the cooking in advance, whereas with a cocktail party, I spend a lot of time in the kitchen putting hors d'oeuvres in and out of the oven. At a sit-down dinner, I can spend more time with my guests. When they are seated in one spot, I can tend to their every need. At a larger party, when the guests are scattered about the house, I'm lucky if I say 'hello' and chat a minute or two with each person. At large parties, I feel as if I'm cheating my guests."

Remember, the "easy way out" may not always be the best. Examine your own "entertaining identity" and decide what's right for you and the friends you want to entertain in your home.

❦ *Before The Dinner Reminders*

1. Follow up telephone invitations with a written reminder. (Review "Extending Invitations" in chapter 2.)

2. Clearly specify *dinner* in your written or telephone invitation. (Review "Briefing The Guests" in chapter 2.)

3. Obtain food preferences. (Review "Briefing The Guests" in chapter 2.)

4. Plan a menu that *you* can cook and serve with ease. (Review chapter 3, "Menu Planning.")

❦ *The Dinner Hour*

Serve dinner no later than one hour after your guests are expected to arrive—that is, if people are invited to come at 7:00 P.M., they should sit down to dinner no later than 8:00 P.M. (earlier, if everyone is there).

If guests are an hour late and have not called, begin eating. If they do call, be flexible. (See "Latecomers" in chapter 11.)

Whether your friends are prompt or not, be sure your dinner is. And, remember, hors d'oeuvres at a dinner party should be light taste-tempters, not a meal in themselves. At one dinner party, the guests started to have cocktails and hors d'oeuvres early in the evening. The food was so filling that the guests asked if dinner could be delayed until they were hungry again. Dinner was finally served at 11:00 P.M. (If you enjoy the cocktail hour more than dinner, then plan a cocktail party.)

Drinks, too, should be light. Since hard liquor dulls the palate, more and more people are serving only chilled aperitif wines before dinner. It has become fashionable not only for gourmet reasons, but because it reduces your chances of having an inebriated guest staggering to your dinner table.

❦ Calling The Guests To the Table

Use a little dinner bell to call your guests to the table. You might consider a dinner bell pretentious, but it does come in handy for getting the guests' attention.

At one party the hostess tried politely to call her guests into the dining room. In lively conversation over their second drinks, the guests didn't hear her appeals. In the end, she had to tap two guests on the shoulders, take them by the hands and usher them into the dining room. The others finally got the message.

Many hosts have trouble getting the guests' attention. By the time dinner is ready to be served, the conversation is usually going strong (as well it should be). A dinner bell does the trick. When the guests hear it tinkling they, more than likely, will interrupt their conversations—either out of courtesy or surprise. Now that you've got their attention, call them to the table.

❧ The Seating Plan

Devise your seating plan in a way that offers the best possible conversational arrangement. Pair guests who will be compatible. Separate the ones who might be antagonistic. Seat old friends next to one another so they can "catch up" on the news. Separate close friends who see each other every day; they will probably relish the opportunity to speak to someone they don't see quite as often.

You may wish to follow the rules of etiquette when arranging your seating plan. The male guest of honor sits to the hostess's right, the female guest of honor sits to the host's right, and couples sit across from, not next to each other. Your guest list need not have an even number of males and females so the seating plan may seat two men or two women side by side.

While I recommend the use of place cards at most dinner parties, for those of you who prefer not to use them on every occasion it is vital that you indicate to your guests where you would like them to sit; do not leave them to fend for themselves. Make a prearranged seating plan in your head or on paper and then graciously direct your guests to their seats. However, for more than six or eight, place cards are really easier.

Place cards do not have to be elaborate and should not be considered pretentious. You can break the formality with a little humor in their design. (Review "Place Cards" in chapter 6.)

❧ Action In The Kitchen

Set a timer in the kitchen that will sound off when a certain dish is finished cooking. There's nothing like a little buzzer to help you politely break away from a conversation when it's time for you to get on with serving the meal. This may seem abrupt but otherwise you might have difficulty excusing yourself.

Joanne told me, "I always set a timer in the kitchen when I know I have to check the food in the oven or on the stove. It used to be that when I was with guests in the living room or at the dining room table, I would get so involved in a conversation that I often forgot to check the food. Even if I remembered, I sometimes found it awkward to excuse myself from my guests. After I overcooked a lot of food, I finally bought a timer. It works like a charm and gets me into the kitchen. When guests hear the buzzer they let me leave immediately."

Once you're in the kitchen, utilize your time efficiently. Maintain order by having serving dishes, platters and utensils ready for use. Section off one specific area for soiled dishes and pots, instead of piling everything haphazardly in the sink or on the countertops. Clean-up is for after the guests leave, but organization is important so that things don't get broken.

Clear the table with a tray. It's practical and time saving. Remember, serving and clearing should look easy. A tray will help you accomplish this and curtail the number of trips to the kitchen.

I know a compatible couple who share the service of the meal when they have a dinner party—Ann serves and Chuck clears. They make the service seem effortless. Whatever system you institute, if you make it look painless, the guests won't feel obliged to assist.

Scrape the dishes *after* they are brought into the kitchen. There's nothing more repulsive than scraping leftovers into one disgusting-looking pile. While stacking the used dishes in a neat pile at the table may appear to facilitate the clearing procedure, mounding the leftovers is ugly and vulgar. Even if there's only a sprig of parsley or a slice of lemon on the plate, wait until you are in the kitchen to scrape the dishes. Sometimes a well-meaning guest begins scraping the dishes and offers to help clear the table after dinner. Politely but firmly decline.

I suggest one practical rule for entertaining at home—"Don't let guests help you." While there are a few exceptions, you can't go wrong by following this rule in general. At a dinner party, the entire table is disturbed when a couple of guests get up to help. In addition, with someone "helping" certain tasks take twice as long. And, if you follow the rule, fewer dishes will break.

So when the guests offer to help clear the table or scrape the dishes, tell them you can manage by yourself. And you can.

❦ Dining In The Truest Sense

Don't just eat, dine. There *is* a difference. Give your guests a chance to savor the essence of the food. In the same sense that a party can be just a party, floating somewhere in the realm of mediocrity, eating, too can be a commonplace function. On the other hand, a party can be a gala and eating can be epicurean bliss.

Don't rush your guests. Allow them to enjoy every bite, every dish, every course. Eating should be an experience, not just an activity. This doesn't mean that you should overdo. Your dinner party doesn't have to be a bacchanalian feast. Remember, understate rather than overstate. Today's dinner parties emphasize quality rather than quantity.

The most popular menus comprise an appetizer, a main course, and a dessert. However, there is no required number of courses; plan as many as you can serve comfortably. Whether you have planned a seven-course meal or a simple main dish and a salad, serve what will be most pleasing to you and your guests. But give them time to enjoy it.

Instead of serving a lot of different dishes at one time, spread them out over a number of courses. The guests will enjoy the relaxed dining and will appreciate the unhurried service. In addition, you will avoid simultaneous, last-minute preparations in the kitchen. (Review "Painless Menus and Service" in chapter 3.)

Time the courses carefully. Be perceptive and look for signs that the guests are finished eating. Use your own good judgment. Guests want to have time to savor the food and the atmosphere yet not sit too long in front of a dirty dish.

One of the major criteria we use to evaluate fine restaurants is the quality of the service. Assuming that the food is good, if our meal is timed properly so that we are neither rushed nor kept waiting too long, we consider the restaurant worthwhile. The same criterion can be used at home. Dinner parties will be successful if you can establish the right sense of timing that lets you dine with satisfaction.

❦ Intermezzo: A Refreshing Extra

Serve a small scoop of sherbet after the first courses but immediately before the main course. Intermezzo, sometimes called *"trou de milieu,"* is a charming little extra.

The purpose of this course is to refresh the taste buds. It's a palate perker-upper. There are differing opinions as to what intermezzo consisted of originally. A popular view is that it was shaved ice sprinkled with a liqueur. It used to be served only between a fish course and a meat course. Today it is most often lemon sherbet, served between the first course or courses and the main course, whatever they may be (not just fish and meat).

Remember, intermezzo is a *small* scoop of sherbet. It can be served in a small goblet, a shallow champagne glass, or a dessert dish. However, it is not dessert. Dessert can still be served after the main course.

Intermezzo is an inexpensive little treat that adds a touch of flair and a gourmet flavor to an elegant dinner. It's meant to delight, refresh and pamper your guests.

❦ Serving Desserts

Follow your instincts with regard to how soon you serve dessert after the main course. Sometimes it's a good idea to ask your guests if they'd like to have dessert immediately or wait a while.

You may wish to serve dessert in another room. Do not, however, have your guests adjourn (while you clear the table) and then come back to the table for dessert. This is too much moving around.

It's important to be flexible in this as in many areas of entertaining. One hostess planned to serve dessert on the patio after dinner. She was about to call her guests from the dining room table. However, she noticed that they were in lively conversation and obviously very comfortable. Rather than break the spell, she let them stay where they were and served dessert in the dining room.

Wherever you serve dessert, remember the "it's not only what, but how" philosophy. Use attractive serving platters, pedestal dishes with doilies, and serve desserts spectacularly.

᭪ And Afterwards

Relax and enjoy the satisfying afterglow of a well-prepared, well-organized, and well-served meal. Don't feel that you must organize a specific activity. After dinner most guests simply like to settle down for some pleasant conversation.

If you like, serve some cordials or dessert wines. You can have these attractively set up on a tray in the living room. Don, an intuitive host, sensed some of his guests were saying, "No, thank you," to an after-dinner drink because everyone else had said "No." To remedy this situation, he made some suggestions as he had done when serving cocktails. "Would you like an after-dinner drink? I'm going to have a glass of brandy. Would you like to join me?" This was enough to put the guests at ease and some of them did join him.

You may love to dance and want to plan some dancing for after dinner. But don't expect everyone to kick up their heels. Do your best to provide the right atmosphere. Rearrange furniture and rugs, if necessary, and put the stereo in a convenient spot. Those who want to dance will join in if the surroundings are conducive.

If you plan games for your party, try to make sure that you invite game-playing guests. Encourage everyone to participate but don't worry if some friends refuse. Let them continue with their conversations and let the game-players play.

In the final analysis, after-dinner activities will depend on your own taste, judgment and flexibility.

❧8

The Logistics
of Service

❧ Styles of Service

Choose the style of serving that is easiest and most comfortable for you. There are three styles:

SIT-DOWN The guests are served while they sit at the table.

BUFFET The food is displayed on a main table. The guests serve themselves and sit at snack tables or use their laps.

BUFFET/SIT-DOWN Guests serve themselves buffet style from a sideboard or server and then sit down to a formally set table.

Before you decide on the style that's right for you, evaluate the space in your home. If your dining room table seats only eight, then restrict the guest list to that number and plan a sit-down dinner. Or invite more people, use your dining room table to display the food and serve a buffet. Do a little furniture rearranging, set up a few smaller dining tables and have a buffet/sit-down.

One style is not better than the next; your choice will often be dictated by the number of people you want to entertain. An intimate sit-down is nice for a small group while a buffet may be the only feasible mode for a larger one. After careful consideration, determine the style that's best for you, your guests and the particular occasion.

❦ *Sit-Down*

Charm your guests with a sit-down dinner or luncheon that you serve all by yourself. There's no limit to the number of courses so guests can dine in the truest sense.

There are four optional methods of service for a seated dinner.

1. *You can sit or stand in your place, fill each plate from a stack next to you and then pass it down the table.* When you start to pass a plate be sure to say, "Please pass this to Mary. This one is for John . . . ," etc. This indication is important in order to avoid having a plate go round and round the table with everyone being too "polite" to accept it. Alternatively, if the plates are not stacked, you can ask each person to pass his or her plate and then return it directly. No matter which way you deal with the plates, this method of serving from your place is good for main dishes such as oven-to-table casseroles that are too hot to be held or for heavily sauced dishes that could easily spill if they were passed.

2. *You can pass the food around the table in serving bowls and platters, family style.* Keep the serving pieces and platters on a server or sideboard.

   A hostess complained, "Whenever I have a seated dinner, there never seems to be enough room on the table for the wine let alone the serving bowls. I end up removing the centerpiece to make more room on the table." This doesn't have to happen no matter what method of service you're using. A server or even just a bridge table with a cloth on it, can hold the large serving bowls, platters and other utensils. A server also makes a convenient spot for dessert dishes, cups, and flatware which are not usually included in a place setting for a dinner. As a result, the table remains attractively set throughout the meal.

3. *You can walk around the table and serve the food individually to each guest.* This method is convenient when you have a platter that is too cumbersome to be passed around from guest to guest. And, it avoids the passing back and forth of plates that occurs in method one. I sometimes combine methods by serving the side dishes family style and taking the main platter around myself.

4. *You can fill the plates in the kitchen and bring one to each guest.* Many apartment dwellers find this method the most suitable because of its space-saving ability. Hosts don't have to worry about serving pieces or servers. In addition, the impact of a prearranged, attractively garnished plate can be very appealing to the eye and the appetite. I find this method very effective for serving cold salads at luncheons.

Over the years there have been different ideas concerning the problem of when guests should begin eating. A comfortable and practical solution is that after a couple of guests have been served a hot dish, the hostess should suggest that they begin. When you are a guest, if your hostess does not make this suggestion, I would advise that at a small dinner (up to six) you wait and at a larger party you begin when served. Of course, you should dine in a leisurely fashion and pace yourself so that, no matter what, you do not finish before the hostess even begins!

After the food is served, the wine can be poured. (When estimating the quantity of wine needed, the general rule is one half bottle per person for dinner.) The host can help each guest to the first glass and then tell them to help themselves thereafter. Jug wine should be transferred to an attractive decanter. That or a bottle or two of wine can remain on the table.

A sit-down dinner or lunch is advantageous to hosts because they can easily look after the guests. While the guests remain seated for the length of the meal, the hosts can see to it that they are comfortable, satisfied and pampered. Having a dinner party with a few special friends is one of the most intimate forms of entertaining at home.

ℰ Buffet

Dine without a dining room by planning a buffet. Ideally, each guest should have some sort of table or snack tray on which to rest his or her dish. Otherwise, laps will have to suffice. However, it is mandatory that each guest have a chair. Expecting people to sit on the floor is fine for teenagers and young children; but, unless your party is extremely informal and you know your guests well enough to know they'd be comfortable on the floor, don't ask it of them. Each person should have a seat and preferably some table space.

A buffet requires good trafficking with a minimum of congestion. The best setup is to position the buffet table in the center of the room so that the guests can serve themselves from both sides. However, if you need more floor space you can situate the table against a wall. The traditional order of buffet items is first dinner plates, then the main dish, side dishes, salad, bread, butter, napkins, and flatware. (And serve food that doesn't require a knife since some guests will be managing their plates on their laps.) Gravies and sauces should immediately follow the dishes they accompany (nothing too runny). Duplicate the same order of dishes on the other side of the table to effect faster service.

For practical reasons this customary order of items is sometimes altered. One host had a large group, over twenty-five people, so he displayed food only on the main table. Dishes, napkins and flatware were featured on another table situated in an opposite corner of the room. This reduced congestion at the main table.

A buffet can be as formal or as informal as you like. It is a flexible party that can conform to the shape and size of your home. You can display food on a kitchen countertop or on a makeshift table in the living room. Guests can serve themselves and then disperse in any direction you wish. Wine can be served to the guests wherever they are seated. You may want to display desserts on a separate table or on the buffet table after the main course has been cleared. Dessert plates and cups can be conveniently kept on a server in the same room until they are ready to be used. If there's not enough room for a server, the dessert utensils can be brought in from the kitchen at the appropriate time.

The terms buffet dinner and buffet supper mean that a full meal is served buffet style. A cocktail buffet is an ambiguous term. If you use it, be sure to define your meaning to your guests. (Remember the problems we discussed in chapter 2 under, "Briefing The Guests.") Preferably, avoid the term altogether.

Buffet style is popular for brunches, bridal showers, christenings, bar mitzvahs, and housewarmings. It is ideal for large groups when you don't want to seat everyone around a dining room table or for small groups when you don't have a table at which to sit.

ℰ *Buffet/Sit-Down*

Set up the platters and bowls of food on a sideboard, server or countertop. Guests can fill their own plates (buffet style) and then take their seats at place settings already arranged with flatware, glasses, and a napkin (sit-down style).

If the first course is served in the living room, be sure it can be easily managed on a plate balanced on the guest's lap. The only way to serve the first course in the dining room is to have it already in place at each setting when the guests arrive at table. When the main course is ready on the sideboard, call the guests to the buffet, let them fill their plates and take their seats again at the table.

For dessert, guests can serve themselves from the buffet and sit down again at the dinner table (which you have cleared in the meanwhile). Or, you may prefer to have dessert set up in another room. Either way is acceptable as long as you don't have the guests move to another room and then back to the table again. (Remember our discussion in chapter 7 under "Serving Desserts.")

Jennie told me about an awkward evening at a buffet/sit-down dinner. The guests had cocktails and hors d'oeuvres in the living room. They got up to go into the dining room, sat at the table, got up to serve themselves the first course, sat again, got up to get the main course and sat again. After dinner the hostess asked her guests to move into the living room while she cleared the table. They sat down for a while and then were called back to the table for dessert. The last haul was back to the living room for cordials! Few guests want to sit in one spot all evening, but a parade such as this is the opposite extreme.

In order to avoid "promenading," limit yourself to serving a main course and dessert with perhaps an appetizer in place, as mentioned above. Your menu is actually not that restricted because buffets traditionally include a variety of dishes that might otherwise be served in separate courses.

Buffet/sit-down dinners are very convenient for many hosts. You need only set out the platters and bowls and guests can help themselves to the size portion they want. Yet there's still a comfortable seat and place setting for each guest at the table. The trafficking can work well. If you like the easiness of a buffet but the intimacy of a sit-down dinner, then a buffet/sit-down is for you.

9

Cocktail Parties

❦ The Endangered Species

Draft your guest list for a large cocktail party as conscientiously as for a small dinner party. The reputations of large parties, particularly cocktail parties, have tarnished in recent years. Why? Because hosts and hostesses have invented the big "Pay-Off" party, inviting anyone to whom they feel socially obligated. They stuff people into a party like cream cheese into celery. Partygoers have rebelled against this "Anything Goes, Everyone Goes" type of party and many times they simply do not attend or, at least, do not look forward to these bashes.

Prudent hosts will evaluate the space available in their home and then invite only as many guests as they can accomodate comfortably—elbow room for everyone.

You can't count on R.S.V.P.s to a cocktail party invitation. Many people will not take the time to respond, possibly because they feel their presence, or lack of it, won't be noticed. However, for planning purposes, the general rule is that two-thirds of the invited guests will attend a large party.

Another factor that has contributed to the downfall of cocktail parties is chitchat. Many people abhor small talk. However, if your guest list includes a balance of serious talkers (and listeners) as well as those who enjoy hopping in and out of conversations, you should be able to create an interesting party.

Intelligent planning can help get cocktail parties off the endangered species list.

❧ Requirements and Timing

Combine quality beverages, fine foods, and a gracious attitude into your cocktail party. Plenty of ice, glasses, cocktail napkins, and ash trays should be on hand, and good ventilation is very important. Greet each guest at the door and try to speak with each one personally for at least a few minutes. If you've planned wisely, people should mix as well as the drinks, and the traffic should flow as smoothly as champagne.

A cocktail party in the purest sense consists of cocktails and hors d'oeuvres. The time is before dinner somewhere between 5:00 and 8:00, lasting about two hours. On the other hand, some use the term cocktail party in a broader sense to refer to a party that begins after dinner, includes cocktails and hors d'oeuvres, lasts several hours and ends around 1:00 A.M. For clarity's sake, I term this an after-dinner party and only use "cocktail party" in its truest sense. The major difference lies in the fact that the after-dinner party takes place *after* dinner and to me it means including dessert and coffee in addition to cocktails and hors d'oeuvres.

Decide the time and length of your cocktail party beforehand, and state it clearly to your guests. If you expect guests to start leaving around 7:00, then specify 7:00 as the time the party ends. Close the bar thirty minutes after that. Late stayers will soon realize that the party's over. However, when you don't want the guests to leave at a fixed time, indicate only the time the party starts.

Guests will note the hours written on the invitation and use them as a guide in making plans for the rest of the evening, such as dinner or a show. This does not mean they will arrive promptly or leave promptly. Expect guests to arrive at least fifteen to thirty minutes *after* the indicated starting time. Some people feel awkward about being the first to arrive although there's no need to feel this way. (Review "Smooth Arrivals" in chapter 4.)

❧ Good Circulation

Never have enough chairs at a cocktail party. Encourage everyone to circulate. Don't allow anyone to sit glued to a seat.

Haven't you been to at least one party where the guests form their chairs into one large circle? As more guests arrive, the unknowing host brings in more chairs. The "sewing circle" becomes larger and larger and these circles produce a single conversation with lulls long enough to put everyone ill at ease. Everyone feels compelled to say something—like, "Isn't this spring weather nice?" or "Is it hot enough for you?" Yawn. Yawn.

If guests are circulating they can move from one cluster to the next until they find an interesting bunch or, at least, the hors d'oeuvres. Provide as much room as possible so that guests can move and mix comfortably. If necessary, remove some pieces of furniture from the living room and store them in the bedroom or enclosed porch. Remember to put breakable knickknacks in a safe place.

Use as many rooms of your home as you think necessary to provide an uncongested atmosphere. For optimum circulation, situate the bar in one room and the food in another. And if there are more than 25 people, two bars in opposite areas of the house are a good idea. Use the living room, dining room, family room, den, and patio or whatever the best lineup of rooms in your home happens to be.

There are two ways to encourage guests to circulate throughout the designated rooms. First, remember that guests will go into *any* room with food in it. Lure your guests into a sitting room or family room by putting some hors d'oeuvres, nuts, or a small plate of cheese and crackers in the room. This lets them know that they are expected to use this area. If guests are not encouraged to move around, they will feel constrained and stay in one place. Secondly, attract guests to the patio or any other spot by arranging cozy conversation areas with facing chairs. On a table between two chairs put a candle or some snacks. If the area looks inviting, guests will accept the invitation.

At a healthy cocktail party, circulation is a life-sustaining factor.

❦ *Tidbits, Snacks, and Canapés*

Emphasize quality rather than quantity when planning your cocktail party menu. "Simple but elegant" is in the limelight now, whether your guest list is comprised of sophisticated gourmets for a formal affair or good ol' friends for an outdoor get-together.

When planning a cocktail party menu, follow the guidelines that are outlined in chapter 3, "Menu Planning." Use your best, pretested recipes. Do as much advance cooking as possible with a minimum amount of last-minute preparation. Arrange a good balance of hot and cold snacks. Three cold and two hot hors d'oeuvres comprise a suitable menu. Cold foods like homemade cheese balls, patés, dips, and gelatin rings can be prepared in advance. Even a large variety of hot hors d'oeuvres can be prepared beforehand, frozen and reheated just before serving.

Consider logistics in the kitchen. If you must have some hors d'oeuvres that require last-minute broiling or baking, at least limit the number. You'll spend less time in the kitchen and more with your guests. Ideally, it is as important for you to enjoy preparing and serving the food as it is for your guests to enjoy it.

Serve finger foods that can be easily handled without a dish. Don't serve anything messy or runny. Guests hold a drink in one hand and have only one other with which to select a tasty tidbit. Don't expect guests to juggle a drink, a dish, a fork, and a cocktail napkin all at the same time.

Display some food in a centrally-located spot such as the dining room table and arrange to have finger foods passed around on trays. For instance, a variety of canapés can be passed among the guests while sliced fresh vegetables, a creamy dip, and a platter of assorted cheeses and crackers might be on the main table. In addition to displaying some food on the main table, remember to place some snacks on tables in all the party rooms for instant nibbling. Good food goes along with a good party.

ℰ *Stocking The Bar*

Stock the bar with quality liquors that are popular among your circle of friends. Guests will appreciate a small selection of first-rate beverages more than a huge variety of inferior brands. Limit the choices but provide the best your budget can afford. When estimating the amount of liquor you will need for a cocktail party, a workable estimate is three drinks per person, but of course, this varies from group to group.

If your friends like bloody marys, then make a batch beforehand. You can offer a variety of cocktails, if you like, but it isn't necessary. Some hosts serve only wine or only champagne. At a Christmas party, guests can sip eggnog or at a "Kentucky Derby" party, mint juleps. Punches are well liked and are particularly popular at afternoon parties and brunches. Hosts serve them because they "go a long way."

Trim the bar with a substantial variety of popular mixers like club soda, ginger ale, tonic and the now-fashionable sparkling mineral waters, if that's your "cup of tea." There are bound to be guests who prefer nonalcoholic drinks, so in addition to the above, you might want to store some juice or cola for them. And, because we live in a sweet-toothed but increasingly weight-conscious society, it's a good idea to have some diet drinks, too.

Many liquor stores will take back unopened bottles of mixers as well as unopened bottles of liquor. So it's wise to have a variety on hand "just in case."

❧ Accessorizing The Bar

Keep plenty of glasses available. Guests tend to "lose" their glasses and take new ones for fresh drinks. As I mentioned in chapter 4, "It's Not Only What But How," use glasses that are fun to drink from. If the glass is fun, the beverage tastes better. And it's always nice to embellish drinks with attractive garnishes.

For practical reasons, many party-givers use plastic cups for large parties since they usually don't have three dozen matching glasses on hand; but liquor stores do. My liquor store offers attractive stemmed glasses with a 12 ounce bowl. I use them for a variety of drinks. If you ask, many liquor stores will lend you, free of charge, as many glasses as you need provided you buy the liquor at their store. All you need to do is return the glasses cleaned (and unbroken). Plastic cups are appropriate for outdoor entertaining, pool parties, and picnics; but, if you're having a more formal party, you might prefer "real" glasses.

Next to stocking enough glasses, having enough ice cubes is important. Start making ice cubes several days before the party, put them in plastic bags and store them in the freezer. If you don't have sufficient freezer space, order ice cubes and have them delivered at the beginning of the party. It's a needless embarrassment to run out. (And try to find something more attractive than a garbage can to store them in.)

A well-dressed bar will always include a cloth for those inevitable spills and a good-size receptacle nearby for empty bottles and cans.

❡10

A Potpourri of Parties

❡ Lunches

Invite friends for lunch on any day of the week except Monday. For many, Mondays are diet days when willpower is strong and expectations high. But by Tuesday the promises of yesterday are often forgotten.

Plan a light meal and guests will relish your tempting dishes. Unless the luncheon is a special occasion or a formal affair, people expect a luncheon to be light. A main course, salad, and dessert are quite enough. Chef salads and gelatin molds are popular and can be prepared in advance.

One hostess, Mariann, told me about her luncheon philosophy. She always prepares a pseudo low-calorie lunch for her diet-conscious friends, and everyone leaves quite satisfied. Her menu includes a salad, such as Waldorf or spinach, and homemade bread or biscuits (a temptation for those who feel they *must* cheat). For dessert she serves an assortment of cheeses or a dessert cheeseball. It doesn't matter if the cheese has as many calories as a slice of cake or if the salad is as fattening as a club sandwich, it *seems* to be less fattening and, therefore, doesn't conjure up as much guilt.

Keep the drinks as light as the menu. Serve an aperitif wine, a light rosé, or dry white wine. Forget the martinis. No one wants groggy guests in mid-afternoon.

Set your table as meticulously as you would for a sit-down or buffet supper. Use a centerpiece but dispense with candles in the daytime. Remember to use place cards for sit-down luncheons and one written menu on a fine piece of notepaper. Guests are just as curious about a menu at lunch as they are at dinner.

Just for fun, assign titles to your dishes when you write the menu. The name can apply to the theme of the party. If you plan a luncheon in honor of a bride-to-be, don't serve just punch, serve Honeymoon Punch. For a baby shower, don't serve just a layer cake, serve a Lullaby Cake. It's corny, but cute.

One noteworthy luncheon was in honor of a friend's promotion to vice-president. The invitations were typewritten in the form of a memorandum. The place cards were typewritten, too, with a paper clip attached to each one. The written menu listed each dish: Board of Director's Quiche, Supervisor's Spinach Salad, and an Executive Fruit Compote for dessert. The new vice-president and the guests got a big kick out of these imaginative touches.

❦ Brunches

Perk lots of coffee and serve it throughout the party. Offer bloody marys, screwdrivers, champagne, or fruit punch. Start your brunch around 11:00 A.M. or 12:00 and end it around 2:00 or 3:00 P.M.

Invite friends who like morning parties and can savor good food, good drinks, and good company even in the morning. Some people find it difficult to converse with one person in the morning, let alone be cheerful enough to attend a party. Some people have difficulty just getting up and out. So play it safe, and invite "morning people" to a brunch.

Traditionally, the menu consists of a meat dish, egg dish, some fresh fruit, and rolls, biscuits, or bread. Casserole dishes and quiches are popular, as well as breakfast meats or fish like sausage, bacon, ham, or smoked salmon. Most brunch dishes can be prepared in advance and kept warm in the oven. Sometimes, however, you can cook one dish, such as eggs, at the last minute. But keep last-minute cooking to a minimum and you'll make things easier for yourself.

At one brunch, Tom, the host, took the role of chef. At the kitchen stove, he prepared omelettes to order. A variety of ingredients was displayed on the countertop. Guests had their choice of cheddar cheese, mushrooms, onions, bacon, caviar, or green peppers. The "house specialty" combined all the ingredients. The chef enjoyed cooking and everyone had fun.

Serve sit-down or buffet style depending on how many people are invited. At a brunch it is particularly important to inform your guests what dishes are coming by writing the menu whether you're serving one course or three. Brunch menus are so varied that friends have little way of knowing what you have planned unless you inform them. (As I mentioned in Chapter 6, don't expect them to count flatware or dishes as a means of guesswork.)

Rosemary told me about a brunch she attended. There was a sumptuous display of mixed fresh fruit, cantaloupe balls and sliced pineapples, plus an assortment of homemade biscuits, croissants, and bagels. There were curls of chilled butter and dollops of cream cheese made with an ice cream scoop. After finishing everything on her plate, she relaxed with a satisfied appetite only to discover that the fruits and breads were merely the first course. Orange-glazed ham, sausage shish kebabs, and seafood Newburg followed; dessert was yet to come. Had the menu been written, Rosemary would have been able to gauge her appetite instead of having to gorge it.

❧ *Outdoor Entertaining*

Entertain alfresco. There's something special about sitting under a shady tree sipping a tall, cool drink in the daytime or dancing under a starlit sky on a warm summer evening. No wonder so many people enjoy outdoor parties.

Many hosts like the advantages of outdoor entertaining.

Simple and easy dishes are the norm. There's usually more room in the backyard than inside. The house stays tidier and the clean-up is easier. Plastic plates, cups, and glasses provide convenience and a casual atmosphere.

Easy entertaining is marvelous but don't let casualness slip into sloppiness. Neatly set tables that are colorfully coordinated and creatively decorated are just as noticeable on the lawn as they are in the dining room. Even though outdoor entertaining is less restrained, it should never be done at the expense of graciousness.

ELEGANT EVENINGS   Dazzle your guests with an elegant outdoor party in the evening. Combine the ease of summer entertaining and the enchantment of candlelight. Surround your backyard with a halo of candlelight. Fill sandwich-size paper bags, preferably colored ones, with sand and put a three-inch household candle into each one. Place the bags one foot apart on the ground along the perimeter of the party area. When the candles are lit, your guests will love the wonderland quality they impart.

On the main table cluster candles of different sizes and on each of the smaller tables use a taper or a votive candle. The combined candlelight from all the tables will have your guests glowing.

Arrange small round tables or bridge tables in a cozy conversation area. Cover the tables with wildly colorful printed cloths. If you're working on a budget, make your own table coverings from remnant fabric. And while you're at it, make matching dinner and cocktail napkins, too. No need to sew; use pinking shears.

Betty, an economy-minded hostess, uses colorful sheets to make tablecloths. She asks, "How many hostesses can afford an ample inventory of attractive *matching* bridge-size cloths?" Not many. So she buys a twin-size sheet, usually on sale, and cuts it in half. One sheet will cover two bridge tables. And with the cost of paper products today, using cloth sheets is less expensive in the end because they are reusable. The "sheetcloths" are washable and need no ironing.

BARBECUES, PICNICS, AND COOKOUTS   Prepare the coals for the barbecue before your guests arrive. That way you won't be kept from socializing.

Terry complained that she never spent enough time with her guests because she was off in a corner of the yard barbecuing the meat which required her constant attention. She solved the problem by setting up the bar in the same area. The bar lured the guests to the barbecue pit and Terry tended to the cooking while she chatted with the guests.

Stock the bar with lots of cold beverages. People get thirsty in warm weather. Have an ample amount of nonalcoholic drinks for teetotalers, as well as beer, vodka and tonic, piña coladas, or whatever happen to be the popular drinks among your circle of friends.

Barbecues are fun and easy and the menu should be, too. Serve cold salads, lots of fresh fruit, and meats that are easily cooked on the grill. Take advantage of the large variety of fresh fruits and vegetables that are in season during the picnic months.

The most popular style of service for a cookout is buffet. Ideally, situate the table under an awning or shade tree to keep the food from spoiling in the sun. After the guests serve themselves, they can take their places around a picnic table or find some other cozy area where lawn chairs and snack trays have been clustered.

Be flexible about the day's activities. Games are fun, especially if children attend the party. Plan a tug-of-war, relay races, or a volleyball game. Invite everyone, young and old, to participate. If swimming is planned, tell the guests beforehand. Advise them whether to bring or to wear their bathing suits. Clearly indicate to the guests the specific activities you have planned so they can prepare accordingly.

Propose a rain date when extending an invitation to an outdoor gathering. If you don't offer a rain date, at least plan beforehand what you will do in case an uninvited thunderstorm crashes your party. Damp weather doesn't have to dampen the spirit of the party. Prepare an alternate party area, such as the family room or playroom. Decide what your second course of action will be and institute it with ease if the situation arises.

Besides uninvited thunderstorms, ants and mosquitoes love to invade outdoor parties. Spray insect repellent *before* the food is brought out; use torches, electric gadgets, or whatever is necessary to dissuade these intruders from upsetting your party.

❦ Children's Parties

Jam pack a children's party with lots of activities. Children love music, dancing, and games. Their attention span is short so don't let any one game last too long. The tolerance of most adults is also short-lived so don't let the party last too long either. Two hours is enough time for both fun-loving children and stouthearted parents.

Let the children make their own party invitations if they are old enough. If not, assist them. When my daughter, Marissa, was four years old we made candles by cutting out four strips of construction paper and pasting them to the cover of the card. Above each "candle" we put a tiny dot of paste and sprinkled glitter to form the flame. I wrote the pertinent information inside the card, addressed them, and Marissa and I mailed them together. This activity was fun for us and the other children loved receiving the invitations in the mail.

Limit the number of guests. Your child shouldn't invite every youngster he or she has ever said hello to in the schoolyard. If you are fortunate enough to have a large backyard and the season is warm, plan an outdoor party. If you live in a city apartment or it's winter time, decide on a reasonable number of guests who can comfortably enjoy the party indoors. Discuss the format of the party with your child and decide on something that is mutually agreeable.

Don't overestimate your own abilities. Ask a friend or neighbor to assist you when playing games and serving refreshments. Children's parties are not known for their nutritionally balanced menus. But junk foods are losing popularity today. Instead of sweet soda and gooey candy, serve apple juice and donuts. You can serve food that children will enjoy without serving junk. If the children are invited for lunch, hamburgers or grilled cheese sandwiches will do nicely.

Along with food, games and prizes play an important role. At my daughter Noelle's birthday party, we tied a rope between two trees in the backyard. Donuts hung on strings dangling from the rope. The children were instructed to line up in front of the dangling donuts with their hands behind their backs. At the count of three, each child had to eat his or her donut without touching it. The first one to finish won the game.

Avoid process of elimination games. When the first child is "out" he or she may feel ostracized and become devastated. Play games where the spotlight is on the winner not the loser (such as the donut game, above). It's easier for a child to accept the fact of not winning when he or she is one among several, rather than being singled out as the loser.

Team games lend themselves to children's parties. For example, divide the children into two teams and conduct a race by having them pass an orange or balloon from child to child under the chin without using hands. The team that finishes first is the winner. Be sure to play enough games so that each team wins at least once—then *every* child is a winner.

Choose inexpensive prizes for each game. Winning matters more than the cost of the prize. All the prizes should be approximately the same size. Children won't believe that "good things come in small packages" if someone else's package is larger.

Some parents have fallen into the "keeping-up-with-the-Joneses" syndrome. This causes children's parties to get out of hand. The reasoning seems to be that a party isn't a party unless you hire a professional clown, rent a pony who is dressed up with a silly hat or engage a person who can twist a balloon into 1001 different shapes. There's nothing wrong with hiring entertainment for a party. But it should be done with the sole intention of pleasing the children. Competing with the neighbors or hiring someone because you can't be bothered with the party yourself is an unfortunate attitude. Concerned parents who are willing to contribute their time and creativity to their children's party can be much more effective than Mr. Balloon. For suggested children's party themes see p. ooo.

&l After-Dinner Parties

Create your own repertoire of menus for an after-dinner party.

A popular format is to serve cocktails and a variety of hot and cold hors d'oeuvres throughout the evening and end with dessert and coffee. A variation on this style is to go lighter on the hors d'oeuvres and then present a late-night buffet such as spinach salad, quiche Lorraine, assorted homemade cookies, and coffee.

Another imaginative option is to skip the hors d'oeuvres entirely and provide a sumptuous array of dessert cheeses coupled with nuts, fresh and dried fruits, and a variety of wines. Your finale could be after-dinner mints and imported chocolates—elegant finger food!

One distinguished hostess with a sweet tooth gave a delicious after-dinner party featuring international coffees spiked with liqueurs. She offered Irish coffee, Italian espresso with anisette, and a Colombian blend with a chocolate cordial. Miniature pastries provided a charming accompaniment.

Since music is the food of love, why not consider it for your party. Organize in advance the records or tapes you want to play. Keep the volume of your stereo down or you'll find people unable to converse without shouting. If you have a friend who has a talent for tinkling the ivories, with a little coaxing, he or she might play and everyone can sing along. For a special occasion you might hire a small combo.

Games are good ice-breakers. At Jane and Joe's party they asked each guest to bring a baby picture. Jane numbered the photos and attached them to a bulletin board. The guests had to figure out who belonged to what picture. Even though all the guests didn't know one another at the beginning of the evening, they were soon laughing and chatting as they began to write down their guesses.

With good food and good mixing your party is bound to be a success.

ꕥ Cooperative Parties

Share the expense of a party by planning a cooperative gathering where everyone splits the cost. This can be arranged with a group of good friends who are willing to share the work. Two popular excuses for not having parties more frequently are cost and effort. If these two factors were divided among friends, there would be many more parties to attend.

Initiate a progressive dinner with friends who live close by. Have cocktails and hors d'oeuvres at one house, the main course at another and dessert at a third. You can enjoy a magnificent meal and the companionship of friends without the burden of cooking and serving everything by yourself.

Start a dinner party group where all the participants share the cooking and the cost. Plan the menu beforehand with your friends. Each person prepares a dish at home and brings it to the home of the host. Everyone keeps track of their ingredients. The expenses are totaled and divided evenly among the group. This type of dinner party will allow you to enjoy an elaborate meal that one person would rarely prepare alone.

Vincent, a gourmet's gourmet, told me of one such dinner that he and his friends enjoyed. "We began with a country pâté and hot Roquefort cheese pastries for hors d'oeuvres. *Coquilles St. Jacques à la Provençale* came next and then the hostess served lemon sherbet as intermezzo. With our palates refreshed, we proceeded to a sumptuous *châteaubriand* surrounded by fresh garden vegetables. After the main course, a piquant change of pace was provided by a watercress and endive salad. Finally, an Amaretto soufflé and espresso topped off the meal."

An ambitious meal requires a good deal of planning plus a group of friends with formidable culinary talents if it is to be a success. Once in a while you might not want to bother coordinating everything in advance and just try a "potluck surprise" with everyone bringing whatever strikes their fancy.

A "Share the Cooking" party is fun, too. If you are blessed with a large kitchen, invite some friends to join in the cooking of the meal. Have all the ingredients ready when the guests arrive. Assign one dish to two people. Later, sit down to the fruits of your work. (Be sure the guests are told that they are invited to cook as well as to eat.)

For friends who appreciate the pleasures of the grape, organize a wine and cheese tasting party. Ask each person to bring a bottle of wine or an unusual cheese. Or select one person to do the shopping then share the cost evenly among everyone. Conduct a taste test and vote for your favorite wine and cheese.

Cooperative parties with good friends who are willing to participate can be great fun, a delight for the tastebuds, and you can entertain more often and less expensively.

❦11
Dealing Diplomatically With Guests

❦ Diplomacy

Treat your guests graciously and kindly. Your guests are special people, special enough to be invited to your home. But, be realistic, too. Awkward situations and problems with certain guests will occur. At one time or another, some guests will be rude and inconsiderate. At these times, prepare yourself to be a diplomat.

I can offer a few methods to help you handle uncomfortable moments. These suggestions are not, of course, a panacea for every dilemma you will confront. Each party, each guest, each host, and each predicament is different. Use your common sense and discretion under all circumstances.

Try to take the spotlight off the guest who arrives late, breaks a glass, or spills a drink accidentally. Turning attention away from these types of situations is a gracious gesture.

Guests are fascinating individuals. Some don't respond to written invitations, some bring uninvited guests or even their children. Some arrive too early, stay too late, or put cigarette butts in your plants. Then there's the one who spills red wine on your white lace tablecloth and the other who asks, "What's in this?" before tasting anything. You may have encountered the guest who announces he is dieting after you've prepared a five-course meal or the one who tells you he eats only margarine when all you have is butter. My favorite is the guest who arrives at the table, blows out the candles, turns on the glaring ceiling lights and mutters, "I hate to eat in the dark."

Thank goodness these situations occur rarely. But when they do, be prepared. How will you respond if a guest breaks an expensive piece of china? What will you say to the person who is causing an argument at the table? And what about the guest who comes to dinner and stays for the weekend? Diplomacy is the answer.

❧ Overnight Guests

Decide in advance how long your houseguests will stay. The length of the visit should be settled before they arrive. Then guests will know they're not overstaying their welcome, and you will be able to plan your menus, prepare your food in advance and organize the activities.

While visiting Marie and Peter at their country home, my husband and I chuckled at a sign that hung on the guest room wall, "If we get to drinking on Sunday afternoon and ask you to stay until Tuesday, please know that we don't mean it."

Tell your guests what activities you have planned and what kind of clothes to bring. "On Saturday afternoon we'll go swimming at the lake. In the evening we'd like to take you to a local restaurant for dinner. Jackets are required for the men." Give the guests as much information about your plans as possible.

Prepare as much food in advance as you can. Carefully plan each meal. Utilize recipes you can prepare beforehand. Your guests' visit will be more pleasant if you spend more time with them and less in the kitchen.

Let the guests help, if they genuinely show a desire. Aside from dealing with shy people, this is the only exception to the rule "don't let guests help you" which I mentioned in chapter 7 under "Action In The Kitchen." Some overnight guests want to feel like part of the family. If you think they want to pitch in, give them a little chore to do. "Tonight, Frank, will you prepare the salad?" Or "Mark, will you carve the roast? You have a knack for it." On the other hand, don't overwork your guests.

Alter the daily chores and other customary patterns around the house if they will inconvenience or take too much time away from the guests. If you usually wash and wax the kitchen floor on Saturdays, let it go the weekend you have overnight guests. Just do the essentials. The house won't fall apart. If you have morning coffee every day at a neighbor's home, postpone it until your guests leave or take them along.

Be flexible in the activities you have planned for your guests. They might not want to participate in everything. Allow time for rest and relaxation and ample time for dressing. Ask your guests what they would like to do. Give them options.

Give guests their own room, if possible. If you can't provide such private accomodations, tell them in advance. If they are agreeable, then don't worry about it. But be sure to give your guests a specific place where they can keep all their belongings. Make room in one of the closets for their clothes. They'll be more comfortable and your house will be kept much neater.

Treat your guests like V.I.P.s. Have special guest linens, fresh towels, a new bar of soap, and a nightlight. Stock the medicine cabinet that the guests will be using with toothpaste, aspirin, mouthwash, shampoo, and one or two new toothbrushes (just in case they forget their own).

Pamper your guests. In the guest room have a bouquet of fresh flowers, a bowl of fruit, and some interesting reading material. Leave a pitcher of ice water with clean glasses on a table in their room. Be sure to have extra hangers in the closet and extra blankets, too.

Your overnight guests will appreciate your effort and will depart with pleasant memories.

❦ Early Arrivers

Don't be thrown by early arrivers. Some people have a tendency to come earlier than the appointed hour so, no matter what the occasion, be ready at least fifteen minutes before your guests are scheduled to be there. Judging the time can be difficult, particularly when people are coming from a distance. If you appear to be ready and waiting for them, their arrival won't seem like an intrusion and they will feel more comfortable.

Greet guests hospitably at the door. Don't embarrass them by telling them how early they are. They usually know. Be pleasant and gracious. You can't very well tell them to go back and sit in the car or wait in the hallway for a few more minutes. Lead them into the party room. Offer to make them a drink or ask them to help themselves.

Excuse yourself politely if it is necessary for you to do some last-minute preparations in the kitchen. Say, "Please excuse me. I'm working on a schedule and will be with you in a few minutes." If they are considerate, they will understand.

Remember the rule, "don't let guests help you" and don't bring them into the kitchen. A simple task like preparing the coffee or filling the ice bucket can take forever with two or more guests crowding the kitchen. You will feel better when all the preparations in the kitchen are complete and the guests are yours to entertain for the evening.

❦ Latecomers

Minimize the inconvenience when some guests arrive late. Introduce them to a few people in the room if the party is large. It's not necessary to introduce latecomers to everyone or call attention to their lateness.

If guests are one hour late for a dinner party and have not called, start serving the dinner. There's no reason to penalize the others for the tardiness of one or two. When the latecomers do arrive you can say, "I'm sure you would have wanted us to begin," as you lead them to the table. Let them take their places inconspicuously and resume normal conversation.

If there are some who display the "come-late-and-make-a-grand-entrance" syndrome, ignore them. And if you have a celebrated friend who falls into the "I'm-an-important-person-so-I-can-be-late" category, cross him or her off your guest list.

If some guests are going to be late and call in advance, be flexible. If they won't be too late, tell them you will wait until they arrive before serving. If they are going to be very delayed, tell them you will begin and keep their portions warm. In the case of a short delay, inform the other guests that you plan to wait. The long details are not necessary. For example, "Claire and David will be delayed a half hour, and I'd like to wait for them before starting dinner. In the meantime, how about some more hors d'oeuvres or another drink."

As I mentioned in chapter 4, "It's Not Only What But How," it should not be expected nor considered fashionable for guests to arrive ten to fifteen minutes late. It's silly to try to figure out what time the host *really* means when he says, "Come at 8:00." Eight o'clock should mean eight o'clock. Guests and hosts should be on time.

❦ Dieting Guests and Fussy Eaters

Serve the food you have prepared for your guests with confidence. If something is refused, don't make an issue out of it. The person may have a good reason for refusing.

Some guests who are dieting don't want you to interfere with their self-control. Hollandaise sauce or cherries jubilee can be very tempting, but if they have made up their minds not to eat, nothing is going to change them. Don't force them. Respect their willpower. (For guests who require special diets for medical reasons see "Eat, Drink, and Be Merry" in chapter 12.)

Then, too, there are fussy eaters who ask, with a turned-up nose and a nasal intonation, "What's in this, anyway?" before they taste anything. Politely tell them the basic ingredients. Then let the decision be theirs.

Catherine told me about a custom in her home when she was a child. When anyone at the table didn't like a particular food that was being served, he or she took a "no-thank-you portion"—a small amount, just to taste. Wouldn't it be nice if we all learned to be so polite?

When you're telephoning invitations or when a guest calls responding to a written invitation, try to obtain information relating to his or her food preferences. This is one way to avoid the embarrassing situation of preparing an omelet for a guest who doesn't like eggs or a pecan pie for a person who is allergic to nuts. You will probably know these facts about close friends, so preparing for them will be easy. But with someone you don't know very well that you sense is a fussy eater, be up front. Ask tactfully, "Are you allergic to any foods." The guest, at this time, will not only take the opportunity to tell you if he or she has any allergies, but will probably mention other foods that are personally distasteful. A guest once told me very concisely, "I don't eat anything that flies or swims."

❦ *Spills, Breaks, and Accidents*

Take the spotlight off the guest who accidentally spills or breaks something at your party. Blame an inanimate object instead. Say, "Those glasses are really top heavy" if your favorite crystal goblet is shattered. If an obese person sits on a bridge chair and it collapses, blame the chair not the weight. Blame *anything,* never *anyone.*

At one of Pat's elegant dinner parties a guest accidentally spilled a glass of wine. The guest's face turned almost as red as the wine. Pat quickly cleaned the spill and diplomatically put the onus on a fold in the tablecloth. That, not the guest, caused the glass to topple. Pat immediately transferred the blame and everyone's attention from the embarrassed guest to an inanimate object.

Another way to ease the embarrassment of a guest who's in an uncomfortable situation is to empathize by saying that you, yourself, have recently done the very same thing (even if you really haven't).

When a mishap occurs, clean it up quickly and quietly. Do what you must to prevent permanent spots and stains. But, do it fast. After you have administered first aid to the rug or tablecloth, dismiss it from your mind. Once it has happened there is nothing else you can do. The embarrassed guest will feel much better if you don't look upset all evening.

❦ Arguing Guests

Change the topic of conversation as subtly as possible if an argument occurs at your party. Use the "segue technique" that radio and television announcers often do. If you see a pointless argument erupting, make a transition from one topic to another. Whether the guests have strongly differing opinions about politics, jogging, religion, pediatricians, or makes of cars, deflect an argument that's heading nowhere by saying, "Speaking of . . . the other day. . . ." Purposely detour the conversation in another direction that is less controversial to those guests.

If the "segue technique" doesn't work and the volume of the argument has reached a glass-shattering pitch, ask the antagonist a question that requires more than a "yes" or "no" answer. Choose the guest who is shouting the loudest and making the others feel uneasy. Ask him a question. Ask about anything. If he takes the time to answer you, he will, more than likely, calm down a bit. This attention-diverter should make him aware of the disruption he is causing.

Change the emphasis of the conversation and purposely go off on another tangent. When a loudmouth states, "All politicians in Washington are dishonest," ask her, "Have you ever been in Washington? It's a marvelous city. The new subway, the Metro, is remarkably efficient." She should pick up the hint.

Realize that some people do enjoy a good discussion. They don't want to waste time on small talk. If a heated debate is stimulating, though controversial, let it happen. You have to judge whether your guests are enjoying themselves or whether they are uncomfortable.

❦ Overdrinkers

Leave a jigger on the bar to be used for measuring when guests are going to mix their own drinks. Some guests are handicapped by poor judgment, either when measuring liquor or in knowing their own capacity.

Overdrinking at parties is a concern to be reckoned with. Here are some ways to approach this problem:

1. Don't force guests to drink. Some guests don't want to seem impolite so they accept a second or third drink when they really don't want it.
2. Store plenty of nonalcoholic beverages that can be served after a guest has had his fill of liquor for the evening.
3. Always serve food with drinks, preferably protein because it stays in the stomach longer.
4. Stop serving alcoholic beverages a while before guests leave. Coffee may help but providing time for the alcohol to be absorbed is the best way to get your friends home safely.

Yet even under the best circumstances there's a possibility that some guests will drink too much. When that happens you can ask someone at the party to drive the guest home, offer to call a taxi or suggest the guest stay overnight at your home.

❦ Shy People

Do all you can to include shy guests in the conversation. Make them feel relaxed. As I suggested in chapter 4, "It's Not Only What But How," when introducing a shy guest to someone else, mention something about each person. Help the shy guest to a first piece of cheese or first slice of cake. Make some suggestions when offering a drink and be encouraging about second helpings.

At a dinner party seat the shy guest towards the middle of the table so he or she can join in the conversation more easily. Seating a shy person at one end of the table may make that person feel left out. A friend who's shy might have just the attentive ear for the stories of another friend who's an excellent conversationalist. However, this type of matching can backfire, so pair your opposites carefully.

At a cocktail party enlist the wallflower as your assistant. (An exception to the rule "don't let guests help you.") Put a platter of hors d'oeuvres in one of his hands and a bunch of cocktail napkins in the other and send him off on an expedition in the living room. He will be forced to chat with the other guests.

A shy person usually just needs a little time to warm up. He or she sits quietly and observes the others, listening and waiting until a favorite topic of conversation comes up. You can hurry its arrival by asking questions, lots of questions. Inevitably you will hit upon some topic of interest.

Genuine flattery works wonders. Even the shyest guest can't resist telling the background of an unusual piece of jewelry or how he keeps looking so fit and trim. Be honest in your compliments, though. Everyone can see through a phony.

❦ Late Stayers

Threaten to show home movies of your children or cats to any guests who stay too late. Travel slides also work well. But, seriously, when guests overstay their welcome, the situation must be handled tactfully. Sometimes plain and simple honesty is best, "I'm very tired and I have to get up early tomorrow."

One friend recommends the "Second Pot of Coffee Trick." She explained to me that as the guests are talking and it's getting late, she asks them if she should prepare another pot of coffee. More than likely the guests will say, "Oh, no thank you. We have to be going soon." That's her cue to stand and start inching her way to the door. It's very important to *stand;* it breaks the spell of the conversation.

If the guests are a stubborn group, resort to more obvious methods. Start organizing dishes and cups on the table. Empty the ash trays. The guests are bound to take the hint. (Do not, however, start a full-scale clean-up or disappear into the kitchen.)

If they still won't leave, just keep yawning or seriously consider the home movies.

❦ Unexpected Guests

Smile. There's nothing you can do about unexpected guests. You may feel inwardly flustered when they arrive. You may even feel like crying. But try to overcome these feelings as quickly as possible. A congenial host is outwardly delighted with drop-in company. And, you may find you are truly delighted by the time the visit is through.

I once told an old friend, Diane, to definitely visit me the next time she was in town. One morning I was preparing for a dinner party for ten people the following day. The phone rang. "I'm in a telephone booth one block from your house. Can I come by?" Of all the days to choose, this one couldn't have been worse. However, I did want to see her so I said, "Certainly, certainly. Give me ten minutes."

Rrrr-ing. There was the doorbell. I cleared my mind of all the chores I had to do and devoted my attention to my friend as we sat talking over coffee. I began to enjoy her visit even though it was inopportune. After a half hour I had to get on with my preparations so I said, "I'm having guests for dinner tomorrow and I've got to begin my list of do-befores." Diane understood but asked if she could stay for a while as she had a couple of hours before her next appointment. We discussed the menu and table decorations and she had another cup of coffee. In the end, I was able to have a good time with my friend and get my work done, too.

Be prepared for unexpected guests by keeping an "Emergency Food Shelf" in your grocery closet. Stock it with cookies, crackers, canned fish and meats, processed cheeses, tooth-picks, and cocktail napkins. Keep your freezer well stocked with precooked main dishes or casseroles, quiches, individual frozen hors d'oeuvres, and cakes. Keep a list of good "take-out" restaurants in your neighborhood. Note whether they deliver and what their best dishes are.

If you have unexpected guests for dinner, don't overload yourself with work and frustration. Serve a dinner that doesn't require a lot of preparation, such as a broiled meat, tossed salad, and garlic bread. Keep a list of recipes which call for ingredients you usually have on hand. I have a recipe of this type for lemon dessert bars. My husband loves these cookies and is happy to see unexpected guests because he knows what the dessert will be.

Unexpected guests shouldn't expect a sumptuous, five-course dinner. But, if you are not ruffled by their arrival, look pleased to see them and are hospitable enough to offer them something to eat, it's a feather in your cap. If you are prepared for the unexpected, you might even be pleased when the door-bell rings.

❦ *An Ounce Of Prevention*

Have foresight and carefully plan your parties. You may notice that I have mentioned most of the following points before, but I will repeat them here to stress that potential problems with guests *can* be avoided and some awkward situations elimi-nated.

Prepare a harmonious guest list. When you are planning your party, avoid inviting guests that will clash. Invite people who are compatible and who have a mixture of interests. They don't necessarily have to know each other. Cross off the trou-blemakers from your list.

Follow up telephone invitations with a written reminder one week before the party, just in case your friends forgot the date. Use written notes with the hope of preventing any confusion regarding the expected time of arrival, especially for early ar-rivers and latecomers. For example, indicate on the reminder, cocktails at 7:00 P.M., dinner at 8:00 P.M. This will prompt those perpetual latecomers who inevitably miss the cocktail hour to arrive on time for dinner. If you want your party to end early, start it early. You will have less occasion to resort to the home movies if you do.

Exchange pertinent party information over the telephone. Acquire information about the food preferences of finicky eaters. Give overnight guests details about their stay. Tell guests the specific mode of dress at your party. In all these cases, you will avoid surprises by discussing the details with your guests in advance.

Provide enough room for your guests and don't overcrowd the party. Never resort to the big "Pay-Off" party that I mentioned in chapter 2 under "Cooking Up The Guest List." Minimize the possibility of accidents by having an ample supply of cocktail napkins, coasters, ash trays, and snack tables.

Plan and prepare as much as you can in advance so that you can enjoy your own party. But realize that the unexpected may occur and, if it does, be ready to handle it diplomatically.

❧12

When You
Are The Guest

❧ Esteemed Guests

Contribute your enthusiasm to a party from the moment you accept the invitation to the time you leave at the end of the party. An esteemed guest is an enthusiastic guest who wholeheartedly shares in the fun. Be agreeable, amiable and obliging. Talk to the other guests. Participate in the party's activities with gusto. If there are games, play them. If there is music, dance. Be an asset to the party because you are the party.

No one likes the ol' stick-in-the-mud who doesn't want to get his bathing suit wet, who refuses to join in when everyone is singing and who didn't have any time to make a costume for the masquerade party.

An invitation is a compliment. Your hosts have thought enough of you to invite you to their home so be courteous, gracious and use your common sense.

❦ R.S.V.P.

Respond promptly to an invitation. You have only to be a host a few times to realize how frustrating it is to still be wondering four days before the party how many people will attend. An efficient host plans and prepares for a party well in advance, a gracious guest responds as soon as possible.

However, if you can't respond promptly, at least respond. Otherwise, it's downright rude. As a guest you must inform your host whether or not you will attend a party, even if it's a large cocktail party and the response seems relatively unimportant. To the host, it is very important. A host must prepare the food, drinks, other accessories for the party. It makes a difference if ten instead of twenty people are coming. A brief telephone call sufficiently informs your host. Another gracious alternative is to write a short note. Sometimes sending a note is faster than making a telephone call.

And when you accept an invitation, accept it sincerely. If you don't want to go to a party for whatever reason, then don't go. Be confident enough to refuse an invitation if you so choose. Don't go to someone's party if you have no intention of ever inviting that person to your home or, at least, continuing the friendship with some sort of reciprocation. However, don't keep a scorecard, either. Social obligations need not be tit for tat, although a thoughtful person does reciprocate.

❦ Entrances

Arrive on time for a party. No, it's not fashionable to be ten minutes late. If your hosts wanted you to arrive at 8:10 instead of 8:00, they should have said so. If you know beforehand that you will be late, tell your hosts. If you are unexpectedly delayed before the party, call as soon as possible. Spare the long stories when you call, but try to find the opportunity to offer an explanation to your host or hostess privately when you get to the party.

If you are late, enter as inconspicuously as possible. Take

your place at the dinner table or around the cocktail table and join the conversation.

I witnessed a boisterous guest's arrival at a party. He was half an hour late for a dinner party and never called the hostess. He charged through the door, hung his coat on the doorknob, headed straight for the kitchen, uncovered a pot and demanded, "What's to eat?" The hostess lead him into the living room and introduced him to the other guests. He proceeded to monopolize the conversation for the rest of the evening. I don't know how the hostess felt, but I would have crossed him off my guest list permanently.

Early arrivals are just as inconsiderate as late ones. Don't bring uninvited guests without informing your host and don't bring your children along unless they are invited. There are parties where children are welcome and there are parties where young people's presence would be inappropriate. If you adopt a "where-I-go-my-children-go" attitude, you won't be going too many places.

❦ *"Should I Bring A Gift?"*

Give a small gift to your hosts if you want to express thanks and appreciation in a tangible way. This is usually an optional but always a thoughtful gesture.

There are several occasions on which gift-giving is expected: when you are the guest of honor at a party, or when you are an overnight or weekend guest at someone's home. A set of guest towels, attractive soaps, placemats and napkins, or a plant are all welcome gifts.

In many circles, gifts are offered at dinner parties, but the gesture depends on the traditions established within each community. Guests shouldn't try to outdo one another by offering overly expensive bottles of liquor or ostentatious crystal pieces. The thought is more significant than the cost.

Edible gifts are appropriate. If your hosts have a sweet tooth, give them a box of their favorite chocolates. If they savor the taste of fine wines, bring a bottle of vintage bordeaux; or if they fancy gourmet food, select a wheel or superbly ripened Brie cheese.

It is the hosts' choice whether or not to serve this type of gift at the party itself. Even if the gift does not complement the menu, wise hosts usually ask guests if they would like their gift to be served, rather than chance hurt feelings.

One of the nicest gifts to offer is something you have made yourself. Bring a jar of homemade jam, a freshly baked pie or a hand-embroidered handkerchief. A sensitive host will value your special effort.

A bouquet of flowers conveys feelings beautifully.

One day as I was putting the finishing touches on my table for that evening's dinner party, the doorbell rang. A delivery boy presented me with a colorful arrangement of flowers from one of the guests I was expecting at the party. The card toasted, "To a lovely evening." It made me feel appreciated and added to my anticipation.

Whether the gift is sent beforehand, brought by the guest or sent afterwards, the thoughtfulness that accompanies such an acknowledgement, while not always expected, is always appreciated.

❦ Eat, Drink and be Merry

Eat, drink, but most of all be merry. Cheerful, amiable guests are welcome at any party. Mix with the other people. Eat and enjoy. A party is not the time to start a diet. Wait until after the party to start depriving yourself. It's downright rude for a guest to sit through an entire meal and refuse every course except the lettuce leaves. If you require a special diet because of medical reasons, it is your responsibility to tell your host beforehand. Then the appropriate menu adjustments can be made and you and your host can eat comfortably.

Remember someone's home is not a restaurant. A host need not provide a choice of four salad dressings. Politely accept what is served. If a particular food is not your favorite, offer a quiet "no, thank you" or better yet, take a token portion.

Incredible as it may seem, it's not only children who sometimes make nauseating sounds when an unfamiliar food is served. In addition, it's not only unnecessary but crude to ask, "How can you eat *that?*" The comment may be unintentional, but it's impolite nonetheless.

Drink moderately at a party. Inebriated people are a nuisance to other guests as well as to the hosts. The hosts have enough to do without a staggering drunk on their hands, on their sofa, or in their bathroom.

Rather, add to the party's gaiety by being a convivial guest who eats and drinks in moderation.

ꙮ *Disasters*

Offer to help clean any spills or breaks you may have caused at a party. Dramatic scenes are unnecessary. Clean up quickly and quietly with the assistance of the hosts.

Have you ever been vacuuming the day after a party, and found a stain on the rug caused by a spilled cup of coffee? Remember this when you're a guest and tell your host if an accident occurs. After the accident has been dealt with, forget about it. Get back into the party spirit. Constant apologies are wearisome.

If you feel responsible because you caused a mishap, send a note to the hosts afterwards, or even send a small house plant or bouquet of flowers. If a broken item is replaceable and it is within your means to replace it, then do so. Otherwise offer a sincere apology the day after by means of a telephone call or written note.

ꙮ *Exiting*

Leave the party as graciously as you entered. Grand exits are in just as poor taste as grand entrances. When you decide to leave, thank your hosts and leave promptly. Some guests start to leave and end up having two or three other conversations on the way out.

Don't start a mass exodus, especially if you are leaving early.

Take your coat quietly and slip out the door. Don't force other guests to feel uncomfortable because they are staying. They might feel obliged to say, "Guess we should be leaving, too," although they would really rather stay. On the other hand, don't leave too late. Consider the feelings of your hosts and how tired they might be after four or five hours of partying.

Whether or not the time is stipulated, if you are a perceptive guest, you will know when to leave a party.

❦ Thank Yous

Earmark a few moments of time to send a written note of thanks to your hosts for the party. They deserve more than just a pat on the back and a handshake at the door. Think of the time and effort your hosts have invested in preparation, cooking, serving, and entertaining, and take five minutes to pen a short note. I don't know any hosts who don't love to receive a handwritten thank you letter, and who don't truly appreciate its sincerity—be it from a best friend or an acquaintance.

Include some specifics in your message. Choose the dish that seemed the most extraordinary and comment on that. It's better than saying, "The ice cream was delicious," unless, of course, it was homemade. If the table setting or the decorations were unusually eye-catching, mention them. In short, try to find something outstanding about the party that you can refer to in your note.

While a telephone call is not a substitute for a written note, it is the next best thing. Unfortunately, even with the convenience of Ma Bell at their fingertips, there are many guests who neglect to telephone a word of thanks. If you feel more comfortable telephoning instead of writing to close friends, then do so. The important thing is to convey your appreciation in some fashion.

In recent years we've overlooked a lot of the old-fashioned courtesies that indicate genuine thoughtfulness. It's time for a renaissance.